If anyone is qualified to write this b[...] academic qualifications and then s[...] [...]ıı ɪhis book works is Helen's no-nonsense, common-sense narrative. She makes complicated things simple; grey areas become bright and she is incredibly talented in asking questions that turn your thoughts on their head. I have learnt an incredible amount from Helen in the last 15 years and will continue to do so until we hang up our work boots.

Sarah Williams, Transformation and Change – M&S

I'm not usually a massive fan of 'self-help' books, but I found Better Than Confidence a really easy read with lots of very practical and actionable tips and ideas. It's a book I know I'll come back to again and again, both for myself and when I'm coaching others.

Monique Knaapen, Talent Development Professional

This book is not only relatable and useful, it offers practical solutions for anyone who doubts their ability, credibility or place at the table, whatever that table looks like for you. You can't just sit back and read this book, you absolutely have to join in.

Peta Young, L&D Professional

Better Than Confidence is fantastically relatable and self-challenging. I have already been able to use some of the great tools in my personal and professional life.

Monika Holliday, HR Business Partner – KFC

Helen has helped me navigate many work dilemmas and always with refreshing honesty and hugely practical advice. It's wonderful that she has compiled her expertise and insights into these pages. I'm delighted I now have a permanent written reference guide of helpful tips to dip into!

Martha Hankins, Debt Advisor – Citizens Advice

If you've ever doubted yourself in a world where it seems everyone else knows what they're doing, this is the book for you. There are so many people I'm recommending it to!

Kirsti Macqueen, Visual Design Manager – Perfumers 1870

I found this book to be an incredibly transformative tool to go from confidence just being a buzzword to being something that I can integrate into my life!

Suzy Oklin, HR Manager – KFC

Helen takes the conversation beyond the wishy-washy demand for 'more confidence' and leads you through a treasure trove of tools to help you think your way to success!

Jo Lipman, Marketing Professional

BETTER THAN

CONFIDENCE

The thinking tools you need
to get the results you want

Helen Frewin

Butterfly House Publishing

Wiltshire, UK

www.butterflyhousepublishing.com

ISBN: 978-0-9956849-2-8

Better than Confidence

The thinking tools you need to get the results you want

British Library Cataloguing in Publication Data.

A catalogue record for this book is available from the British Library.

For Jacqueline.
Thank you, Mum, for giving me a soft cushion to land on
when I fell and all the freedom I could wish for,
so I could fly.

Contents

Foreword

Some speakers you can spot from an early age. They are the ones whose teachers had trouble getting them to stop talking. The ones with school reports that say things like, "Nigel has great potential, but it looks like he'll have to find a job where he talks a lot to accomplish anything."

You could say they exuded confidence from an early age, and what got them into trouble then is what propels them into success now.

I was not one of those children. My school reports consistently said that I lacked confidence and needed to speak up more. My careers assessment suggested I'd make a good librarian and I don't think any of my teachers would have predicted that I'd now be mainly talking for a living – advising leaders, connecting with strangers, pitching my expertise, speaking on stages across the world, and being interviewed by the likes of Forbes, HuffPost and CNN as an award-winning author.

I don't know what kind of child Helen was, but the first time I met her as a fellow speaker, I was struck by her gravitas, clarity and presence. She's one of those people you meet about whom you think, "Oh, she's definitely got it all together."

Her presentation held everyone's attention, got us all laughing, nodding and leaning in to know more. I was impressed with how much useful insight she shared in just 15 minutes. This was a woman who knew her craft.

But what sealed the deal for me was how she did all this with connection, not arrogance. As the host, Helen had the additional role of making the rest of us – the speakers and the organiser – look good and, more importantly, making the audience feel good. Helen didn't just appear confident in herself, she instilled confidence in those around her too.

Which is why I was surprised when she first told me she was writing a book with the message that you *don't* need more confidence!

Is it because she's already blessed with plenty? No. It turns out Helen is human – just like the rest of us! She has her doubts, her uncertainties, her gremlins. But she also has something that she will tell you herself is *better* than confidence.

What Helen has pulled together here, with her wealth of experience and in her signature no-nonsense, no-ego, practical and relatable way, is an immensely useful toolkit.

Whatever the outcome you want – whether it's speaking up, making better connections, delivering better results or something else – take this toolkit, play with it, run with it, and enjoy where it takes you.

Grace Marshall
Head Coach, Chief Encourager, Productivity Ninja
Author of the award-winning *How to be Really Productive*

Preface

"You need more confidence" is one of the most useless, vague and unhelpful bits of advice or feedback that exists.

What do we do with it? Take a pill? Wait for a few years, assuming we'll be more confident then?

And, perhaps even more worryingly, this is also something we tell ourselves. Have you ever told yourself that you need to have more confidence before you can do something?

I'm here to tell you different.

Yes, confidence is great. It feels good, helps us to be calm and in control. It can even lead to a better night's sleep.

The problem is that making confidence your goal is a total distraction. It turns your thinking inward to how you feel, which moves you away from the thing you wanted to do.

There are better ways of getting results.

Instead of focusing on how you feel, which is essentially what confidence is, it is better for you to have useful thinking tools that drive you to get the outcome you want.

And the great news is when you use these better thinking tools, not only will you get results, you'll also feel good.

Confidence becomes the side-benefit of better thinking.

If you're reading this book because you think confidence could be helpful for you, take a moment to consider: what do you want that confidence for? Is it just to feel good about yourself?

I doubt it.

Everyone I work with who believes they need to work on their confidence wants to do so because they believe this will help them achieve something else.

My point is simple: start with the something else, not with confidence.

When we focus on achieving our goals, being great at what we do and having a positive impact, we are more likely to succeed. The tools in this book will help you do just that.

It is not the mountain we conquer,

but ourselves.

Sir Edmund Hillary

Introduction

This is the bit where I'm supposed to tell you why I am qualified to write this book. Why you should read it. And I am filled with gremlins – those nasty little voices telling me I'm nobody, I have no right to talk to you or expect you to read this book.

Maybe that's why I'm qualified to write it.

Because in spite of those gremlins, here we are together, and you *are* reading this book. My lack of confidence has not stopped me.

A bit about me, as you might want to know whose advice you're reading... I have spent my entire career over twenty years helping people and businesses get better results.

It is amazing to see what a difference it can make, to give people and teams better thinking tools to work through their challenges.

Jamie was a marketing professional I worked with early on in my career. He was brilliant at what he did but lacked confidence and was missing out on career growth as a result.

After a few workshops and coaching sessions, I didn't recognise Jamie. He walked taller, spoke up with authority, apologised less, and there was an air of calm to him. Anyone looking on would say he had become more confident, but that had not been the focus of his development. It was the side benefit of giving him space to think more effectively.

A global bank CFO came to me for help when executive meetings ran over for hours and achieved little in the way of decisions and action. I offered to facilitate a meeting and within 90 minutes, the team had scrapped projects that were no longer needed, decided on a better structure for the business and planned action for keeping future meetings so efficient. That is the power of better thinking: it changes behaviour and outcomes.

Over the years as a business psychologist, executive coach and facilitator, I have worked in-house in people/HR teams and externally as a consultant, advising on selection and development. These days, as a director at consulting firm Totem, about a third of my time is spent on recruitment-related projects: job analysis, competency frameworks and advising companies on how to select the best people in a more objective way.

The rest of my time is spent on my passion: developing people. Management and leadership development programmes, personal effectiveness workshops and coaching at all levels. I have the privilege of working with some great companies like Disney, KFC and Dyson, and the wonderful people within them.

Teaching people better ways of thinking has been my life's work: helping people speak up in meetings, come across as more confident, apply for that promotion and get it, lead teams more effectively. It's one thing running workshops with twelve people or standing on stage in front of a crowd – in these settings I can get a sense of the impact I've had by the feedback I get afterwards. *"Life-changing"* is a common comment, and then come the emails, weeks and even years later, that bring goose bumps to me every time. Here are a couple of examples:

"I have realised I have been keeping myself small, which is not serving me and is not the person I want to be as a role model to my daughter. I have left my job, started my own business and I am thriving. I cannot thank you enough."

"After hearing you speak, I changed my thinking and spoke to my partner about our issues. We got married shortly after that and have never been happier."

The work that is most rewarding for me, though, is the one-to-one coaching – helping someone wrestle with their gremlins, find the tools that work best for them and then see the transformation. That is an incredible privilege, and it has enabled me to hone and refine the tools I share with you now.

We all experience anxiety and fear at some point in life: some of us more than others. And I have found simple ways for you to work through those limiting feelings and achieve the outcome you want.

Confidence, or a lack of it, need not be a barrier to you shining, unlocking your potential, being your best self – or just getting that crappy thing done that you keep putting off. Having no confidence or feeling like an imposter need not be a problem to you at all. I'll show you how.

But I'm getting ahead of myself. Before we dive into the practical tools, there is a bit of exploration and myth-busting to be done. It's probably useful to start by defining what we mean by confidence in the first place.

"Self-doubt, [...] insecurity and a general sense of terror are completely appropriate...
no, more than appropriate,
necessary for good work to get done."

Dani Shapiro

PART 1

Confidence is Not the Goal

1

What is Confidence?

One of my favourite activities in a confidence workshop is to ask people what they believe is the difference between feeling confident about a task and not feeling confident about it.

What do you believe you would be saying to yourself if you did not feel confident?

What do you believe you would be saying to yourself if you did feel confident?

Here are the most common responses I hear:

"If I were not confident, I'd be telling myself I can't do it. Worrying about all the ways it can go wrong. Remembering times before that I've made mistakes or failed."

"If I were confident, I'd be saying 'I've got this, I can do this.'"

But that's not really true, is it?

Think about a time recently when you have been doing

something you had confidence in yourself to do well. Cooking your favourite meal, tying your shoelaces, having a meeting with a team you find easy to work with, reading a bedtime story to your niece... What were you saying to yourself?

Nothing.

At least, nothing about your level of belief in yourself.

When we believe in ourselves and feel calm, we tend to get in the zone and think only about doing that thing well.

We focus on cooking a great meal, getting the recipe right, the objective of the meeting and how we achieve it.

Confidence then is not a sickening list of positive thoughts about how great we are. I would call that arrogance or narcissism.

Confidence is better observed by a lack of something else. A lack of worry, a lack of fear, a lack of unhelpful negative thoughts like "I can't do this" and panicking what-ifs like "What if I look stupid in front of my colleagues?"

For the purposes of this book then, let's use the following definitions of confidence:

Being confident is a sense of calm, a lack of worry or concern about our ability to succeed.

Being unconfident is the concern that we can't do something, the fear of failing and the worries about what could go wrong.

And let's be clear that over the course of a day, maybe even within one hour, we will complete some activities we feel confident about and some that we feel unconfident about.

Now we have some definitions to work with, let's do some myth-busting. You have probably been led to believe that a lack of confidence is a bad thing and having confidence is a good thing. I'd like to challenge that thinking.

2

Is Confidence Always Helpful?

A lack of confidence is not universally a bad thing. Have you ever been so worried about an interview or meeting that you prepared for every eventuality and did a brilliant job as a result?

Likewise, having confidence is not universally a good thing. Have you ever been so relaxed and calm about doing something that you got complacent and didn't do your best work?

To be confident or not to be confident is not the question.

The question is, "What thinking would be most helpful for me right now to get the outcome I want?"

If confidence is not always helpful in getting the best outcome, then we need better thinking tools.

Let's explore in more detail how the two ideas of helpful thinking and confidence can link, in a 2x2 grid. Because what business book could exist without a 2x2 grid?

This is a grid of how confidence and helpfulness of thinking can show up in any given situation.

How Confidence & Helpful Thinking Can Show Up

	Low **Confidence** High

	Confidence	
High **Helpful Thinking**	**Unconfident Helpful** Concerned Preparation	**Confident Helpful** Calm Preparation
Low	**Unconfident Unhelpful** Staying Small	**Confident Unhelpful** Complacency

Unconfident and unhelpful

Some typical thoughts when you're in this space are:

I can't do this.

It's better not to try.

What am I doing here?

What if I look stupid?

What if I fail?

And the impact of that thinking is often that you don't try. This is part of the brain's natural mechanism to protect you from harm. By not trying, by staying small, avoiding risks, you stay safe. But at what cost? What opportunities have you missed out on?

Unconfident and helpful

Here's the great news. You can take that lack of confidence and simply shift your thinking in a more helpful direction. Common thoughts in this space are:

I don't know if I can do this. How could I prepare so that I give it my best shot?

I'm worried I'll fail. How can I plan for things that might go wrong, work to avoid those things and also respond to them if the worst does happen?

I can't do this. But I want to do this. So how can I make a start?

Negative thoughts are translated into solutions.

Your lack of confidence does not need to hold you back. The anxiety and worry can fuel good questions and helpful thinking that drives you to put in the work and do your best. You might succeed, you might fail, but you can learn from that too. This line of thinking helps us find courage and give things a go, teaching our brain that we can be safe and try new things. Even when we get knocked down, we can choose to keep going. We will be okay.

Confident and unhelpful

Let's see how confident thinking is not always helpful. Imagine feeling really calm and in control: what could be the downsides? Here are some common phrases I've heard from people in this space:

I feel good.

I am not having any worries or fears come to mind about this.

I can just rock up and do my thing. I don't need to prepare, I can wing it.

That last phrase gives the strongest indication of where this can go: complacency. When you feel so relaxed about something, you might spend less time preparing. You might not consider what someone else needs from you, or how you could do the best job. You turn up expecting things will be fine, and maybe they are, or maybe something goes wrong. And you're not prepared for it. It's a risk.

Confident and helpful

Notice the difference here. You can feel calm and still do the work.

I feel calm and have no worries. Now, what outcome do I want?

How can I prepare in the best way to get that outcome?

What do I need to be ready for, e.g. risks that could affect me delivering that outcome?

You put in the work and do your best. Your confidence has not led to complacency.

~~~

Can you recognise situations where you have had each of these combinations?

When I'm running workshops with titles like 'Imposter Syndrome' and 'Leading with Confidence', most of the delegates will share that they have experienced a lot of the unconfident thinking. Sometimes they are in helpful thinking, sometimes unhelpful, but mostly in unconfident. That makes sense, as they have chosen to attend a confidence workshop!

If you have not heard the term 'imposter syndrome' before, this is the name given to that sinking feeling we get when we don't think we are qualified or knowledgeable enough to do the things we're doing. Maybe we think we have been promoted beyond our level of capability. We cannot believe that our success is deserved or that we can achieve what is expected.

The fear is that we'll get found out. Someone will realise we're a fake, an imposter, completely incapable of the job we have taken on.

Imposter syndrome, like a general lack of confidence, can be turned into helpful thinking, which drives us to be prepared and do the best job we can.

For me personally, it is the mix of confidence and helpful thinking that does not come naturally. When I'm lacking fear and anxiety, I am more likely to fall into complacency. I am feeling calm and relaxed, so might not think so much about what I want to achieve or what could go wrong. I have to remind myself to take a moment and think, "What outcome do I want?" and "What could I do to be best prepared to achieve that?"

Helpful or useful thinking is better than confidence because it drives us to action. Confidence looks more appealing; for example, I imagine I would sleep better the night before a big event if I had that sense of calm.

But the reality is that, having worked with hundreds of coaching clients and witnessed them move to a more helpful thinking space, the feeling of calm came from the practical. It wasn't simply self-belief that made the difference, it was doing the work. The preparation and contingency planning led to feeling more in control.

What we see here is that confidence, or a lack of it, is less important than the usefulness of our thinking. So the message we give ourselves or others to "be more confident" is not helpful at all, because it does not help us identify the more useful thoughts that will enable us to succeed.

I have written this book to give you all the tools you need to move to more helpful thinking and be brilliant. Brilliant at what? Well, that's down to you.

The tools in Part 2 could help you have difficult conversations with your family or give feedback to an underperforming team member. Be prepared to ask for that promotion you were convinced you'd never get or find the courage to start dating again.

As long as you can identify the outcome you want, the tools in these pages will help you get there. And if you're not sure what you want, there are even tools here to help you clarify that.

For now, it's time to explore how you might have been using a lack of confidence as an excuse. It's painful challenge time.

3

The Great Excuse

Do you sometimes use your lack of confidence as an excuse?

Yes, I'm going there.

You may have been holding yourself back for years, using your lack of confidence as a reason to stay small.

I'm not confident enough to do this.

I'm not confident enough to try.

Because sadly, that's what your brain will naturally do for you – keep you focused on fear and anxiety and staying safe. If you never try anything, you can never fail. If you never go for that promotion, you'll never have to face the disappointment of not getting it. If you don't speak up in meetings, nobody can ever accuse you of saying something stupid. Say nothing, do nothing – that is the safe option.

And it gets worse, because every time you stay safe, every time you avoid that scary thing, you prove your brain right.

"See!" our brain shouts at us, "I told you not to say anything and not to go for that new role and look! Now you're safe, nothing bad has happened, and all is well. Always listen to me, I'll keep you safe!"

When we follow the advice of our survival instincts and fear, our world can get smaller.

I remember, early on in my career, feeling sick before a team meeting because I had an idea I wanted to share, but I thought it might not be well received. It felt like a huge conflict in my mind. To speak up and possibly do well, versus the fear of being seen as stupid for sharing a useless idea.

After a couple of hours of this to and fro, I remembered the painful truth about how fear works. I realised that if I gave in now to this fear and did not make my 'Big Scary Announcement' (otherwise known as simply stating an opinion), then next time would be even harder. And maybe eventually I would not speak in meetings at all, and maybe then I would not be asked to attend meetings. I could play this out and see my world – and my career – getting smaller.

And now I had the benefit of more balanced thinking. Because the fear of speaking up was now less significant than the cost of not speaking up: the fear of my world getting smaller and me becoming stagnant in my career.

I spoke up.

And let's not sugar coat this. It did not go well.

My voice was shaking, I was spoken over twice, I managed to reassert myself to share the idea and then it was pointed out to me that the idea would not work.

The purpose of this story is clearly not to say, "Feel the fear and do it anyway and everything will be perfect." It's more like, "Feel the fear, do it anyway, experience the bad times and struggles along the way, learn from that and you will have benefited."[1]

I benefited hugely from that experience.

I learnt that being spoken over need not stop me from coming back to what I was saying.

I learnt that doing a bit of homework before the meeting and running my ideas past a couple of people first could have made all the difference.

I learnt that my colleagues could say an idea would not work, simply because it had been tried before. Which gave me the

---

[1] If you have not already benefited from reading about Carol Dweck's research on the Growth Mindset and you are interested in this line of thinking, then I highly recommend this as your next read. *Mindset: changing the way you think to fulfil your potential* by Dr Carol S Dweck is a great book for us all, and particularly interesting for parents, as Dweck considers how we build a growth mindset in our young people too. I've also put a summary of Dweck's research and findings on helenfrewin.com if you want to read an overview.

drive to find out *how* it had been done before and explore whether it could be done better next time.

On the drive home from my 'Great Achievement of The Day', I felt proud. I felt powerful. Like I could choose to do other things that scared me too and know that I could survive, learn, adapt.

And I purposefully chose this story to share with you because it is a small thing. This was a team of five people, only one of them more senior than me. I find it a bit embarrassing that I found it so hard.

But that's the thing with fear. It often turns up in the strangest of places and we tend to believe things will be worse than they turn out. And even when things do go wrong, we get on with it.

How has this fear effect played out in your life?

When have you turned down an opportunity or chosen not to do something for fear of looking stupid or being rejected?

And how has that made your world smaller?

This is one of my bugbears with confidence. We use *not* having it as an excuse.

Well, that stops today.

Confidence is no longer your excuse.

Confidence is not a prerequisite for your success.

You just need some better thinking.

4

Why Are You Here?

As we close this section on exploring confidence and the idea that there are more useful things for you to work on, it may be worth pausing to consider why you are interested in this topic.

The message of this book is: start with the goal you want to work towards and focus on making that happen, rather than getting distracted by your own levels of self-belief.

When we chase after confidence, we lose focus on the thing we wanted to achieve in the first place.

Take some time now to consider why you want more confidence, or what result or outcome you want.

Maybe you want to go for that big scary promotion you've been putting off, because you're not sure if you're good enough. Maybe you simply want to speak up more in meetings or contribute ideas to projects.

Focus on these outcomes as we move into Part 2 and the

thinking tools that will help you get the results you want. And, as an added bonus, when you get your results you're likely to feel more confident too.

"It had long since come to my attention that people of accomplishment rarely sat back and let things happen to them. They went out and happened to things."

Leonardo Da Vinci

PART 2

Thinking Tools

5

Overview

Now we get into the practical. Seven thinking tools to drive you to action and the outcomes you want.

I invite you to treat this part of the book like a buffet, seeing what works best for you.

The ideas that strike you as useful, and things you could try – why not bookmark these chapters to keep coming back to? Once you've had a go with a few, you could build your own toolkit.

There is a summary at the end of each chapter, with reflection questions and space for you to take notes. This may be the most useful part for you, as you can return in future to your own reflections. It's your coach in a book.

To get you started, here is an overview of all the thinking tools:

Better Than Confidence is…

Being Outcome-Focused – Chapter 6

Confidence might mean you feel good about yourself, but a focus on what outcome you want is better. When you know exactly what your destination is, it's easier to get there. Use the questions in this section to clarify what you want and why that is important, and you'll find you're already closer to achieving your goals.

Being Others-Focused – Chapter 7

Unhelpful thinking or a lack of confidence stems in many ways from our concerns with ourselves; our worries about how good we are and what we believe. But what if we made it about someone else? What if doing a good job is all about my team? Or my audience, customers, people I serve? This will shift your thinking to doing the best job you can, not because that will make you feel good, but because you care about someone else and how they benefit.

Being Brave – Chapter 8

Our brain is naturally protective, often reminding us to stay in our comfort zone so we can stay safe. If we wait until we feel confident, we will never act. And so, we need courage. To step out of that comfort zone – whether for you that's a huge leap, or a small step, both take the bravery to act. This chapter gives you a process for identifying your steps to take.

Being Prepared – Chapter 9

A lot of people talk about feeling confident when they feel more prepared. That's usually to do with 'knowing my stuff' – for example, the idea that I can give a better presentation if I am the expert. Yet this chapter is about a different kind of preparation. It's about preparing to manage your fears. What if I fail? What if I look stupid? These are not helpful questions, they are fears. And fears need managing. Confidence might feel good, but if you have not addressed the potential risks with what you're doing, then you're missing an opportunity. It's basic risk management.

Being Challenging – Chapter 10

Sometimes our fears are deeper, linked to long-term unhelpful beliefs. Fear of failure and perfectionism can be extremely limiting to our courage. This chapter is about challenging such unhelpful beliefs. What if you believed failure was part of the learning process? What if you recognised the inherent downsides to perfectionism? We will explore redefining what a good job looks like and choosing more helpful beliefs.

Being Competent – Chapter 11

One of the issues with confidence is that it is subjective. It is my opinion of my level of ability. I feel confident if I *think* I am good at something, regardless of how good I actually am.

Getting more objective can help us to be clear on the level of knowledge, skill and performance we have, compared to what we need, and then build on it. And that's far better for our results than just working on how good we feel about our ability. Stop worrying about how good you *think* you are and start getting better at what you do.

Being Credible – Chapter 12

When the result you want is in any way dependent on communicating with and influencing others, it will do you a few favours, even if you don't *feel* confident, to at least *look* confident. The great news is there are some simple thoughts and behaviours you can practise that will make the difference. These subtle changes will help you have more authority and credibility, which will mean you are more likely to influence others effectively.

An alternative

If you're keen on diving into a specific challenge, then an alternative is to jump straight to Part 3. In that section, we explore the most common scenarios my clients have faced where they thought they needed more confidence.

Speaking up in meetings and presentations are the top two by far. Then we have difficult conversations, applying for a promotion/new job/pay rise and responding to feedback – the classic challenges where you might imagine confidence could be useful. I share which Better Than Confidence tools my clients have found most useful in those scenarios.

Let's dive into the thinking tools that are Better Than Confidence.

6

(Better than confidence is...)

Being Outcome-Focused

One of the most powerful and incredibly under-utilised tools we all have at our disposal is asking questions. Whether you have negative and confidence-limiting thoughts or not, questions are the helpful thinking tool that can drive you towards a better outcome, in a better way.

The most powerful question to start with is:

What outcome do I want?

I warn you now, because of the importance of this question, you'll see it repeated throughout the book. If this was the only thing you took from the whole book, that would be no bad thing, because focusing on what you want is the most helpful starting point.

Being outcome-focused is better than confidence because it moves your thinking away from how you feel about yourself to what it is you actually want. And the amazing thing is that this clarity on what you want is often more than half the battle to achieving it. That's because identifying success measures can often lead to greater clarity on how to get them.

One of our unhelpful tendencies is to talk about what we don't want.

I don't want people to think I'm rude.

I hope he doesn't think I'm a nag.

I don't want to get this wrong.

I'd hate it if they thought I was incompetent.

All this thought and energy going into what we do not want. Have you ever noticed that sometimes all the worry about *not* coming across a certain way seems inevitably to end in exactly that outcome?

A motorcyclist friend told me, "It's just like when I'm on the bike. You have to focus on where you want the bike to go, and not get distracted by things you want to avoid. As you approach a turn, you need to be aiming for the exit of that corner. When you focus on avoiding the issues *within* the corner – curb, manhole cover, debris – you unwittingly end up steering towards those things. Focus on where you want to go, not on the things you want to avoid."

What if we put our energy and focus on what we *do* want?

What difference could that make?

Davide is CFO of a large not-for-profit organisation and I started coaching him when he had just moved into the role. Six months in, Davide was leading a challenging project where more than half of the department was against him. Changing systems and processes was likely to mean that many of their jobs would be redundant in a few years, so this was hardly a popular choice. Davide was about to lead a department-wide meeting where he needed to get people engaged and involved in delivering this transformational change, and he was lost. "I don't want them to ask me about their jobs. And I'm worried they're going to fight me on this, challenge why we're doing it."

I asked him, "What outcome do you want?" He had to stop and think. He had been so focused on what to say and how to lead the meeting that he didn't have an immediate answer.

After a few moments, it started to flow. "I want them to see that this change is good. Even if it does mean that in four years, they might lose their jobs, that's four years away. Right now, they have the opportunity to change systems and processes that are frustrating and inefficient. And we're wasting money. And going through this is a great experience for their career development. There is a lot of good and I want them to see that and *want* to be a part of it."

Would confidence have helped Davide lead that meeting?

Maybe. But being clearer on the outcome he wanted transformed his thinking. He built an agenda that included getting people into small groups to come up with ideas on how they could benefit from being involved in the project, and what they thought could make it run more smoothly.

Clarifying your thinking on what you want is a gift to yourself. It's always harder to achieve something if you don't know what you're aiming for.

If you're thinking about something specific like a project or a difficult conversation, the following questions will help you get that clarity.

What's important to you? Could you list what is most important to you, in general and/or about this specific situation?

Ask why a few times. Why am I doing this? Why is that important? And why is that important?

This can help us get to something that is more emotive and more personal. When we feel more heart-led about what we are doing, it can drive us more towards courage and help us overcome fears, because we believe in our purpose.

Being Outcome-Focused is the first and most critical thinking tool, because it gets us unstuck. Instead of worrying about how confident we are or how competent we are, we shift our focus to what we want, to what's important.

Summary & Reflection

Being Outcome-Focused is better than confidence because it moves your thinking away from how you feel about yourself to what it is you actually want.

What outcome do you want? What is important to you about that? Why is that important?

Make it specific to your context, e.g. what outcome do you want from speaking up more in cross-department meetings?

Or what do you want people to do as a result of your quarterly update presentation? What do you want them to think? Feel?

What's important about that? And why is that important to you?

How would you know you had achieved this? What would be different if you got the outcome you wanted? Any success measures? Again, you could add why these things are important to you, to help you engage with these points at a more emotive, heart-led level.

7

(Better than confidence is...)

Being Others-Focused

One of my favourite moments working with my colleague Krush was when she had a lightbulb moment of, 'It's not about me, it's all about them!' Krush and I had been working on a project together for a few weeks, and it was getting time for Krush to take on the delivery of workshops on her own. Krush knew this content; it was her expertise and something she was hugely passionate about. So I was confused when she sounded so unsure about everything.

"What do I say with this slide?" and "What do I say at this point in the workshop?" were the questions she was asking, only hours before running the workshop solo. I was concerned – had we not prepared enough? Did she not know what she was doing? But that simply wasn't true – she knew this stuff!

I explained that knowing what to say was not about the slide or our prepared agenda, it was about connecting with the audience and seeing what they needed. "But what if I say the wrong thing?" Krush replied.

As we talked through it, I understood that Krush's fears were about perfection. She wanted to look perfect, say everything perfectly and do a great job for me, so that I looked good to our client. Perfectly positive intentions.

But those positive intentions were driving her inward.

Krush reflected on the session we had just co-delivered, which had gone well from my perspective, but she was not happy. "I can do better than that," she told me. And then, with a burst of energy, she said, "It's not about me, it's about them!"

"It doesn't matter if I stumble over a slide or repeat myself or skip some content, as long as they get what they need."

And that was that. She had no more questions, no more concerns. Krush went on to run those workshops brilliantly, enjoying the process, and she got incredible feedback from the client.

The very thing Krush wanted – to be perfect and look good in front of the client – was almost stripped away from her, because she made that her focus. As soon as she shifted the focus to doing a great job and delivering what the audience and client needed, her original hopes were achieved naturally.

What if you stopped worrying about what people think of you, whether they thought that was a good idea, whether you looked stupid just then... and focused on how you can help, how you can do a good job?

What if you made it less about you and more about the people you want to help?

Delivering a workshop on this with teachers was hugely inspiring, because for them this perspective shift took them straight to the children. One of them shared, "I've realised it's not about me looking like I know what I'm doing, it's about the kids in the classroom and how I can help them shine."

Deborah, a musician, composer, teacher and business owner, talked to me about her difficulty in getting the money she needed to do her work. We connected online after she saw a few of my YouTube videos, and started talking about her challenges. When she needed to request funds, she felt uncomfortable. Deborah would find herself thinking, "Who am I to ask for funding? What makes me think my work is so important?"

I asked the question, "What if this wasn't for you? Who could it be for?" and her response brought tears to my eyes.

Deborah's passion is to give others a voice. To inspire people to find their voice. She knew her work did this so when requesting funding, she was now doing it on their behalf. She was asking for funding so that others might find their voice and have the joy of expressing themselves.

Once you have this clarity on who can benefit or who you are doing something for, it is great to consider how you can add value. This is the critical build. You know what outcome you want, and you have some idea of who that is for. But what value can you add to achieve that outcome? To serve that person?

It's always lovely when a business I've been working with for a while says, "We love working with you; we'd like you to work on this new project too..." And yet sometimes this can lead to a big confidence wobble for me. Andrew, one of my clients, was impressed with some facilitation work I had done previously and he asked me to lead a development workshop for the senior sales leaders in the business.

My mind jumped to all the reasons I could not do this – I have never considered myself to be great at sales, I am not a sales expert, these people have worked in sales for decades, each one of them sells more in one deal than I sell in a year, I don't know enough, I have nothing to contribute. You can hear my panic!

Thankfully, I have learnt this lesson enough times that I was able to switch my thinking quite quickly. I say quickly – it may still have been a few hours before I realised I was disappearing into a negative spiral, and I needed a way out.

The two questions that massively shifted my thinking were:

What do they need? And what value can I add?

I started considering who these people were, what they were struggling with (based on Andrew's brief) and how my skills and knowledge might be able to help them.

My thinking shifted to this being all about them.

Instead of focusing on all the things I didn't know, or imagined the sales team knew better than I did, I focused on what I did know. I started listing on paper all the knowledge, skills and experience I had that could in any way be relevant to this piece of work. And that meant going beyond sales expertise, because it's my skill in helping people change their behaviour, try new things and discover better ways of working that could be most useful of all.

When you feel lost, like you can't do something or you don't know where to start, think about what you do know. What experience have you had that could help you? What does this person/team/project/audience need? What skills do you have that can help with that?

I know from my own experience and countless coaching clients that this can end up feeling like a battle. A battle between one voice in our minds saying, "Okay, I know about X and I'm good at Y," shot down by another voice that says, "But you don't know loads of other things and you can't do this!"

It's worth keeping at it. Imagine it's a training exercise for your brain to get used to thinking about what you do know and the ways you can add value. Not to make you feel better, though that can be a side benefit, but to help you take action.

Focusing on what you don't know will drive you to do nothing, or simply panic.

Focusing on what you do know, what your audience needs, how you can help them, how you can add value – that drives you to action, preparation and doing the best job you can.

In the days leading up to the sales workshop, I kept falling down the rabbit-hole of "I can't do this, I don't know enough," and I had a fear of being asked, "What's your sales track record, why should we listen to you?"

Each time, I brought myself back to those questions. What does this team need? How can I help them? What do I know? How can I add value?

The workshop was challenging, but fun. A lot of the sales leaders seemed keen to show me that they already knew all this stuff and that they didn't need to change. And that's where my coaching and facilitation skills added more value than any sales expertise, in asking, "What do you want to achieve? And can you reach those goals doing the same things you've been doing so far?" Now they were with me and wanted to explore ways to hit their stretching new targets.

Nobody asked me who I thought I was to be teaching them, or what my sales track record was, but it had helped me hugely that I had prepared myself for that worst fear (something we'll cover in the Being Prepared chapter).

The great thing about focusing on how you can add value is that it leads to doing a better job *and* feeling more confident: double win. It is a great way to distract ourselves from any negative thinking, like listing all the things we don't know. Imagine next time you are telling yourself you don't know enough and there is X and Y that you just don't know, you could switch to saying, "Okay, but what *do* I know?" If you have started with being others-focused, then you have an idea of who you are doing this for and what might help them. How can you add value to them?

A final thought on being others-focused is whether you could make this even more personal.

What if you were doing this for your best friend? Your daughter? Your brother? A loved one?

I find this comes up a lot in CV-writing and any form of self-promotion. So many of us are uncomfortable with selling ourselves so we do ourselves an injustice. The question, "How would you write that CV if you were writing it for your daughter?" has produced incredible changes in applications. I once saw a business leader go from detailing a few things her team had done to describing how she had led the team to deliver fantastic results. We are often more willing to fight for someone else than we are to fight for ourselves, so if this appeals to you, use it.

Summary & Reflection

Being Others-Focused is better than confidence because it gets you out of your head. Instead of spiralling inward, focusing on how good you are, or at best feeling calm and in control, asking who this is for helps you deliver the best outcome for someone else. This is service at its best. It shifts your thinking to *doing* a great job instead of *worrying about* doing a great job. Focusing on what you know and what value you can add is better than confidence because it drives you to identify how you can help. It is the first step towards achieving the outcome you've just identified you want.

Think about something you're working on.

Who is it for? Who benefits? How do they benefit? And how could that mean even more people benefit?

_____

_____

_____

_____

_____

_____

_____

_____

_____

What do they need?

_____

_____

_____

_____

_____

_____

_____

_____

What knowledge, skills and experience do you have that could add value to them?

_____

_____

_____

_____

_____

_____

_____

_____

_____

_____

As an alternative question, maybe for CV writing, asking for a pay rise, writing your profile for a dating site… How would you go about this if it was not for you, but for someone else that you care about?

8

(Better than confidence is...)

Being Brave

Sometimes we just need to do something. To act. Instead of waiting for confidence or the right time, take a step. Or a leap.

Being brave is better than confidence because it drives action.

How many of us have said we're waiting until the kids are grown up before we try that new career, or waiting until things have settled down at work before looking for a new job? That last one always gets me. When do things ever settle down?!

I'd like to suggest that today is the day to stop waiting and start doing.

I was heartbroken to hear of a friend's nephew who has been labelled in the family as lacking confidence. When he was younger, he was very shy, did not want to try new things and kept himself to himself. And his family supported him, keeping him safe.

Now this kid is a teenager who can't take a bus or a train and, as a result, can't get a job. The label of 'no confidence' has been used by him to stay small and used by his family to keep him safe. They drive him around, do the scary things for him, all the while telling him he needs more confidence.

Instead of telling him he needs more confidence with no clarity on what that means or how to work on it, the family could have a greater impact by helping him take brave moves – even if they are tiny steps. Let's take the example of taking a bus. What if we set our young man the challenge of finding a bus timetable online and working out how to read it? Then we could review his progress and check he is reading it correctly. We could go to a bus stop together, getting him to do the work of planning where to go, what time to catch the bus and where. We could wave him off as he gets on the bus, knowing all the time that if anything goes wrong, he can step off and give us a call to come and pick him up.

Helping people step out in courage is far more powerful than letting their fears rule. And it is natural for us as people who care – parents, managers, teachers – to want to save people from that discomfort. So, here's a challenge to you: fight your urge to keep yourself and the people you care for safe, and instead help them learn, stretch and grow.

Author Dani Shapiro puts this brilliantly in her blog on

doing what scares you:

Confidence is highly overrated. Show me a confident writer, and in all likelihood, you will also be showing me work that falls short of originality or greatness — because originality and greatness come from the willingness to take risks. To leap into the void. To do what scares you. And while it may seem that this leap would take confidence, what it really takes to leap is courage. Which is a whole other kettle of fish.[2]

Have you convinced yourself that you can't do certain things because you're not confident enough?

What if today was the day to challenge that?

What would be one small step you could take now to help you realise you can do this?

Sometimes they're small steps, sometimes they're huge. But we don't know what is on that path until we start walking it.

And if there are specific fears you need to address that are making you feel you just can't take that step yet, then read on. The next chapter, 'Being Prepared', will help you manage those fears and work through them.

When simply starting seems like the hardest thing, I always remember some wise words a mentor, David Newman,

---

[2] https://danishapiro.com/on-doing-what-scares-you/

shared with me...

If you want to ride a bike, you don't sit at home reading manuals about how to ride the bike. You get on it, you give it a go, you fall over, you go again. It's the same with stepping out on a new journey. You can't simply analyse it from an armchair and read manuals on it. If you want to know what your journey could be like, you need to take a step and see what happens.

How to identify your steps

Based on your outcome reflections from the Being Outcome-Focused chapter (page 47), you should have a good idea of what you want to achieve, and maybe also some success measures. Have you got a timescale in mind too: a deadline?

Now work backwards.

For you to get that difference or outcome, what would happen just before that?

And before that?

And if you don't know, then who could you ask to help you make a plan?

This was the process I went through in writing this book. I didn't know how to write a book! But my publisher did. Ellen asked me when I wanted to have a book in my hand, and then she worked backwards, step by step, until we worked out I had just two months to write the first draft.

Panic set in.

Two months?! But we worked backwards again, breaking down how many weeks we had, a word count target for each week, and planning when in each week I would write. Job done.

You will have experienced this too every time you have done something new that was relatively complex. Ever bought a house? Learnt to drive? Filed a tax return? We look at the end goal, particularly when we don't know or understand the steps to get there and think it can't be done. But you did it.

If you want to achieve something where you don't know what the steps are, having someone who knows the process to talk it through with would be very helpful, so you can work backwards from the goal to the first step.

You may find the opposite is more helpful for you. Starting with your first steps. Once you know the outcome you want and you feel stuck, like you can't do it, start plotting out the first few steps to get you well on your way.

How many tasks and projects do we put off, worried about how hard they will be or how long they will take? Yet once we get started, it's not so bad. Once we are in motion, it is easier to keep going. Identifying your first steps and cracking on with them gets you in motion. Make a start.

Summary & Reflection

Being Brave is better than confidence because it means you are doing something. Confidence can be an indicator that we are in our comfort zone, playing it safe. Brave action says we are stepping out, stretching ourselves, maybe a little, maybe a lot. You are growing and learning when you give yourself the opportunity to try something new.

Is there anything you have convinced yourself you can't do because you're not confident enough?

_____

_____

_____

_____

_____

_____

_____

_____

_____

_____

_____

_____

_____

What if today was the day to challenge that? What would be one small step you could take now to help you on the journey towards what you want?

_____

_____

_____

_____

_____

_____

_____

_____

When you feel like you can't do something, or you're not sure how, take time to answer these questions.

How can you do this?

_____

_____

_____

_____

_____

_____

_____

_____

If it's easier, work backwards from your desired outcome. For you to get that difference or outcome, what would happen just before that? And before that?

_____

_____

_____

_____

_____

_____

_____

And if you don't know, then who could you ask to help you make a plan?

_____

_____

_____

_____

_____

_____

_____

_____

Or if you prefer to work the other way around, what are your first steps to get you on the journey towards your outcome?

9

(Better than confidence is...)

Being Prepared

Could we save ourselves a lot of time by shifting our language? Instead of believing we need more confidence, it could be better if we just worked through our fears. I say this because when we start paying attention to our thoughts and the negativity that we might describe as a lack of confidence, it is often fear that is circling around our mind.

What if being prepared for something meant more than just having our content and our train tickets? What if being prepared meant working through our specific fears? Then we would be fully prepared in our mind to effectively manage anxiety.

Suri told me on a presentation skills workshop that she knew she needed more confidence and positive thinking for her to be a good presenter. "Tell me about the negative thoughts you have when you need to present," I asked. And Suri launched into a load of 'what if...?' questions.

"What if I say something stupid? What if there are people in the room who know more than I do? What if I get asked a question I don't know the answer to? What if I get so nervous I forget what I'm supposed to say?" These are extremely common thoughts.

We ask ourselves the question, "What if...?" without answering it.

Why is that?

Because these "What if...?" questions are not questions at all. They are fears masquerading as questions.

It would be more accurate if we were to express these fears as they really are, for example:

"What if I say something stupid?" = It would be humiliating if I did or said something stupid. I can picture people's faces as they judge me and think I'm incompetent. People laughing at me. It makes my skin crawl just imagining it.

"What if I fail?" = I am worried about failing. I don't know what it would say about who I am as a person if I can't achieve this. And that scares me.

"What if she disagrees?" = I hate conflict. I feel so uncomfortable in disagreements. I feel strongly about this thing I want to say, but if she disagrees with me, I have no idea what I would say next. And then I would feel bad for starting an awkward conversation. And then maybe our relationship would break down. That could even affect my career prospects. I'm better off keeping quiet.

What I'm highlighting here is that we often express a fear as a question when we do not mean it as a question. It seems we are not asking the questions to explore what we would actually do if that scary thing happened. And that's a missed opportunity.

It's also a risk management fail. If you were a project manager or business leader and you identified risks, would you just leave them festering in your mind? Imagine a business leader identifying a risk in their market like, "We're losing customers every year and we're no longer competitive on price," and then doing nothing about it. Just lying awake at night thinking, "What if the customers keep leaving?!" It makes no sense. When we identify a risk, we need to do something about it.

Could this be helpful for you – to change the way you think about negative thoughts and fears as good risk management?

One of the most empowering things we can do, one of the great ways of feeling more in control when we feel fear, is to work through our worst-case scenarios. Because when we do this, we move from feeling paralysed by our fears to having an action plan of how to manage them *if* they become reality.

Being prepared is better than confidence because this way you are actually ready to handle your worst fears becoming a reality.

An incredibly powerful way to work through fears has been laid out by Tim Ferriss, in his guide to Fear-Setting. It's a great TED Talk if you fancy hearing the back story of this author and business guru.[3]

Let's look at the process Ferriss describes.

For each fear, plan out how you can mitigate against it. Which means asking, for example, for the fear of saying something stupid: "What can I do to reduce the chance of me saying something stupid?" or, if it's more helpful, "How can I reduce the impact of me saying something stupid?" This last question is particularly helpful because it can help us realise that our fears are not so scary after all. Maybe I can reduce the impact by being less concerned about my fear and focusing more on my audience. Because what's really so bad about saying something incorrect or stumbling over my words when I can simply put it right and move on?

Next, we consider what we would do if the worst happened. If our fear became reality. For example, if my fear is that I'll apply for a promotion and not get it, then what would I do in that situation? Maybe I can put in all the hard work and preparation to apply for a promotion, *and also* be proud of

---

[3] Rather than putting a YouTube link here, which could change, I advise you just type "Tim Ferriss Fear-Setting" into Google and you can find the video.

myself if someone else gets it. Maybe I can be open to learning from the experience. And in the aftermath of "What will I do if that happens?" I could consider the importance of building a relationship with the person who got the promotion and making sure I don't become one of those negative people who tries to sabotage the new leader! I could even decide to look for a job externally if I believe I am ready for the step up.

As an added bonus, Ferriss recommends the question, "What is the cost of doing nothing?" This brings amazing balance to all those fears, reminding us why we wanted to do the thing in the first place. We tend to focus so much attention on what can go wrong that we forget why we wanted to do it in the first place. We need to re-balance that.

I once worked with a business owner who had put off giving someone difficult feedback for *fifteen years*. Can you imagine?! This employee was toxic, causing other members of the team to quit over those years and clients to leave the business. If I could have met this business owner years earlier and asked, "What is the cost of you not addressing this issue?" I wonder if she might have realised the pain and taken action.

One delegate on an 'imposter syndrome' workshop shared that this question was the big eye-opener for her as she realised she was making herself small and letting herself down. Worse, she was not being the role model she wanted to be for her daughter. That was the kick she needed to take action.

What is the cost of you not having that difficult conversation?

What is the cost of you not applying for that role?

What is the cost of you not speaking up in meetings?

This can at least bring balance to what is usually a heavily swayed set of scales saying, "Don't do it, it's scary and it could go wrong!" Now we bring the balance of, "But what if doing nothing is just as bad or even worse?"

What about anxiety?

Sometimes we don't have specific fears in mind, we just have a general anxiety. I tend to feel this in my chest and in my hands. Butterflies in my chest and twitches in my fingers. I'm not thinking about a specific fear or 'what if…?' It's just a feeling. And just like fear, that anxious feeling can get in the way of us doing what we want and doing our best. What if we could change our relationship with that anxiety so that we felt calmer and more in control?

Doing that would be better than confidence because we would be prepared to deal with anxiety whenever it came up in future. In Part 1, we looked at the idea that we have different levels of confidence about different things, in different situations. This means that relying on confidence to get us through new and uncomfortable situations is unlikely to work. But being able to manage fears and anxiety is a process we can work through at any time. We'll be prepared.

There is a general narrative in western society that negative feelings are bad. Feeling sad, lonely, anxious, bored, worried... these are, for many of us, bad experiences that are to be avoided. But at what cost?

Telling ourselves we should not be experiencing anxiety is likely to make the anxiety worse. And trying to push past the anxiety and pretend it's not there could mean we miss out on the opportunity to do something with it.

What if we believed anxiety was useful?

Many people tell me that sometimes those butterflies in the stomach give them a push, an excited energy that spurs them on and helps them do well.

That's the difference it can make if we believe the anxiety is helping us rather than hindering us.

I've seen people tie themselves in knots, lost in a spiral of despair. For presentations, it sounds something like this:

Oh no, I'm nervous. This is terrible. If I'm nervous I'll be shaking and my words will come out wrong. Everyone will see my hands are shaking.

Oh, this is awful! I'm going to look like a wreck; I feel like a wreck.

Why do I get so nervous? This is so not what I need right now.

This has gone from bad to worse! I don't even think I can remember what I'm supposed to say now!!

What if we could shift this to, "I'm nervous, good! A bit of performance anxiety to help me do a great job." Or: "Oh, I'm feeling anxious. Well, that just shows how much I care. This is really important to me."

Follow such relaxed thoughts about anxiety with some of the questions we explored earlier, and you've got yourself a great presentation. What outcome do I want? What value can I add?

If my two suggestions above are way too cheesy for you, like 'feedback is a gift' and 'failure is an opportunity to learn' (both of which I believe, by the way, but such statements do not resonate with everyone!), then here's an alternative.

"I feel anxious. That's okay."

Acceptance Commitment Therapy (ACT) is a relatively new approach in counselling where the therapist helps us accept our negative feelings rather than fight them. Drop the struggle, drop the fight against anxiety and accept it. "I'm feeling some negative stuff, I'm remembering times this has gone wrong before and I'm feeling like I don't want to do this. Okay. That's fine."

Now what? Once we have accepted our negative feelings, we need to commit to something, otherwise we can stay stuck in the negativity.

This is where the outcome question comes in handy again. Because the idea with ACT is that you commit to taking action in line with your values: the things that are most important to you. Asking, "What outcome do I want?" and "What can I do to achieve that?" can help us focus.

To tap into your heart-led, meaningful motivation, you might want to take this to a deeper level, reflecting on, "What is my long-term aim in doing this?" You might hit on things like providing for your family or making a difference to the people you serve.

This links in to Being Others-Focused, as when we take action to serve people we can feel more inspired and driven to succeed than if we were doing it just for ourselves.

This combination of acceptance and commitment is so powerful because it reduces the hold that fear and anxiety have on us and drives us to action.[4]

---

[4] If you are interested in learning more about Acceptance Commitment Therapy, there is an outstanding book that explains the concept clearly and helps you put the ideas straight into action: *The Illustrated Happiness Trap* by Russ Harris and Bev Aisbett.

Summary & Reflection

Being Prepared, by having specific steps to manage fear and anxiety, is better than confidence because you have a process to work through whenever you need it. You are actually prepared to handle your fears if they become a reality, which could *feel like* confidence whilst also giving you practical steps if the worst happens. This is also good risk management; a great skill to build for all sorts of roles, not least project management and leadership.

Think about something specific you want to do but have fears about. Use the table below to list your specific fears and then work through the questions.

Here are some example fears I've heard a lot over the years. What if I fail? What if I don't get the job? What if I ask for the pay rise and my boss says I'm not worth it? What if this relationship doesn't work out? What if I end up having to start again? What if this career change doesn't make me any happier?

What is your specific fear? Write out what you are worried about happening.	What could you do to reduce the chance of that happening, or reduce the impact of it? List as many options as you can.	If the worst happened, and your fear became a reality, what could you do then? List as many options as you can.

Having done all that, now make some notes on the question: what is the cost of you doing nothing? Of not doing that thing you wanted to do?

You may not need confidence; you may just need to realise that the cost of doing nothing outweighs the scariness of what you need to do. And that may drive you forward to do simple things, and amazing things.

What if you could accept anxiety, rather than fight it?

What if you could then commit to doing things that would help you achieve your goals?

_____

_____

_____

_____

_____

_____

_____

Think of a specific situation where you feel anxious. What if you accepted that anxiety was natural and part of the process? How does that change the way you feel?

_____

_____

_____

_____

_____

_____

_____

Now, thinking about what's important to you, and what outcome you want in that situation, what action do you want to take?

_____

_____

_____

_____

_____

_____

_____

_____

_____

_____

_____

_____

_____

_____

_____

_____

_____

_____

10

(Better than confidence is...)

Being Challenging

I'm not talking about being challenging of others here, I'm talking about challenging our own beliefs.

If you have ever considered that your lack of confidence could stem from your childhood, upbringing or a particularly critical teacher, you would not be alone.

It's one thing to manage fear and anxiety in each situation, but what if we've got deeper beliefs that are getting in the way of our success? We're going to explore two beliefs that can really mess with our thinking: fear of failure and perfectionism.

Fear of failure

When it comes to fear of failure, I feel extremely blessed. I am very thankful that my parents brought me up with the message that as long as I did my best, they were happy whatever the outcome. I never had a fear of failure, only a fear of what would happen if I didn't try my best! Whilst that was my upbringing, I have worked with so many people who grew up with a very different message from their families, where it was all about getting the best grades, the best results, no place for second best and so on.

Whether that was your family upbringing or your particular form of fear of failure has come from a different direction, the fact is that we need to acknowledge that these beliefs we have about failure may be our truth, but they're not necessarily *the* truth. What is the universal truth about failure? Is there one? Is failure always bad?

A lot of business literature in the past decade has preached the message of failure being good: if we're not failing, we're not pushing hard enough. We're not taking enough risks. Of course, it depends on your work, right? You wouldn't say those things about a brain surgeon. But there is no doubt that the fear of failure holds us back from trying things that could be beneficial. Taking that job opportunity, asking for that promotion, recommending this business decision with its associated risks. Failing in these instances is likely to provide learning, if we're willing to take the risk, be courageous, do, maybe succeed, maybe fail, learn from the experience either way.

This is not, of course, about aiming for failure. It's about aiming for what we want, what we believe is right, what we think will add most value. Accepting that failure in the pursuit of those things might be worth it. And, most importantly, it is not about if we fail, but what we do with the failure that matters. How we learn, how we talk about it, how we share.

I recently heard a coach share a story about her upbringing, where her father asked her every day what she had failed at. It wasn't about encouraging failure but encouraging a stretch outside of the comfort zone. "If I wasn't failing, then I wasn't pushing myself or having a go at something new. I was missing out on a new experience." We may well challenge that failing at guitar lessons at age ten is a little easier to cope with than failing in our first leadership role. But what if our attitude to failure made all the difference? What if we could be a bit more daring, whilst at the same time doing everything we could to monitor progress, learn and improve? That would make it less likely that we fail.

There is huge benefit in us looking at more healthy and productive beliefs around failure. The questions that may be helpful to you if you have a strong fear of failure are:

How has your belief about failure or fear of failure helped you during the past? What has it protected you from? How has it helped you feel safe and secure?

How has your belief or fear limited you in the past?

What new beliefs would you like to have about failure?

Perfectionism

My friend Tim is a perfectionist, and when he had kids and realised this was going to be an issue, he said to me, "But what's the alternative? Making everything mediocre?!"

There is a significant challenge with telling someone that perfectionism is unhelpful. Because if you are a perfectionist, then you'll most likely have evidence that it has benefits. You probably find you get more work done than your colleagues, make fewer mistakes than your peers, and have a far neater life and home than others. But at what cost?

For a start, as a psychologist I can estimate your therapy bill will be higher. How's that for a cost?!

You get frustrated that other people don't care as much as you do and wonder why people don't put the time and effort in that you do. But what has all that care, time and attention cost you? Your time for yourself? Your wellbeing? Your relationships?

How might your focus on control, a classic side effect of perfectionism, affect the way you're perceived at work? Often our control leads to inflexible or rigid thinking and behaviour. And with most organisations talking about the need to be agile, innovative and adaptable, this could be getting in the way of your success.

There is also the frustrating cycle of perfectionism where,

rather than reaching towards something positive (i.e. a perfect outcome), perfectionists end up focused on the very thing they most want to avoid: a negative outcome or judgement. Perfectionism keeps us self-absorbed, engaged in perpetual self-evaluation. And that leads to non-stop frustration and could go further, to anxiety and depression.

If you relate to these themes on perfectionism, then you may want to consider how you became this way. Because you were not born a perfectionist. No three-year-old stops a parent putting their scribble of a doodle on the fridge because it's not perfect. So, when did you become a perfectionist?

Consider the pressure we place on our children to succeed. Without the social skills in place we might have as adults, children often perceive that pressure as criticism. As though the message is, "You need to work harder, because you're not good enough. And if you're not good enough, I won't love you." It is this perceived criticism and threat of losing the affection and love of our parents that works its way into our mind and becomes a set pattern of thinking.

I am not always a fan of digging into the history and causes of our beliefs and behaviours, as I find that sometimes this can lead to further challenges. For example, if I were to realise that I am a perfectionist because when I was a child I believed it was only by being perfect that I could get affection from my dad, does that help me? Or does that make me wonder what more I can do now to gain affection from my loved ones – and send me down another unhelpful spiral?

That said, this section may have brought up some difficult experiences and realisations for you. Finding a counsellor or therapist to speak to could be a very helpful next step.

You could also spend time here moving towards more healthy and helpful beliefs and behaviours.

What can you do to overcome the drawbacks to perfectionism?

Remind yourself of some more realistic truths e.g.:

"Nobody is perfect."

"Everyone has a bad day sometimes."

"Making a mistake means I am human. We all make mistakes."[5]

Encourage playfulness in your thinking process. Rather than being super serious and fearing failure, what if you were to think of the situation as a chance to play? To create? How might that shift your perspective?

---

[5] I was delighted to hear from a couple of people who read this before it went to the editor that I made a mistake in this sentence. How great is that?! I wrote: "Making a mistake *mans* I am human." Well, now I know for sure, I am human. That's reassuring.

Practise accepting imperfection from others as well as yourself – you might want to have a look back at the section on Acceptance & Commitment in the Being Prepared chapter (page 75) to help with this one too.

Another practical tool here is to challenge the belief, just like with failure. What do you believe about being perfect? What do you believe you gain from being perfect? And lose from not being perfect?

How do you measure perfection? I ask this question because perfection is often described as unattainable, meaning we set ourselves up for immediate failure when we aim for it.

My friend Tim, saying that aiming for anything other than perfect means we accept mediocrity, has a challenge here. Because if perfect is not achievable then we are always aiming for failure. And so, we simply must aim for something else. How about excellent? Or very good? How might we know if something is very good?

This also ties in with getting a more objective view of your performance, which we look at next in the Being Competent chapter.

Summary & Reflection

Being Challenging of your beliefs on failure and perfectionism is better than confidence because it starts to address the root causes of your fears. Shifting these limiting beliefs could open up the opportunity for you to take more courageous steps and push towards more of what you want.

How has your belief about failure or fear of failure helped you in the past? What has it protected you from? How has it helped you feel safe and secure?

_____

_____

_____

_____

_____

_____

_____

_____

_____

_____

_____

_____

_____

How has your belief or fear limited you in the past? What opportunities did you turn down or not go for? How has this held you back from sharing ideas, speaking up and making decisions or recommendations?

_____

_____

_____

_____

_____

_____

_____

What do you believe about being perfect? What do you believe you gain from being perfect? And lose from not being perfect?

_____

_____

_____

_____

_____

_____

_____

What new beliefs would you like to have? For example, how would you like to think differently about doing a good enough job? Or when you make a mistake? Or fail?

_____

_____

_____

_____

_____

_____

_____

If you believed these things, what would you do now?

_____

_____

_____

_____

_____

_____

_____

_____

_____

11

(Better than confidence is...)

Being Competent

Everything I have said so far is pointing in this direction. Just get better at what you do rather than worrying about how you feel about yourself!

Being Competent is better than confidence because competence delivers results. Confidence says "I think I'm good at this," whereas competence, and building more of it, gets the job done.

You might think this means diving into improvement, but we first need to identify *what* we need to improve – because we may not be accurate in our views of what we're good at and what we need to work on.

How are you judging your ability? Is your assessment accurate? How do you know?

I find many of us are too reliant on other people's views or, more likely, our perception of their views. We're so often obsessing about what other people think about us when the fact is, that person we're worried about is probably obsessing over what other people think about them!

What if we could be less reliant on what we think other people think of us, and get a more objective sense of how good we are?

From there, you can identify strengths and development areas. And in case you're stuck in the old mindset of always needing to work on your weaknesses, let me challenge that.

It is when we focus on our strengths that we can achieve amazing things. Instead of focusing your energy on improving something you find difficult, draining, even painful, why not focus your energy on the things that energise you? That's what a strength is – not just something you're good at, but something you enjoy and find natural as well. When we're doing something that gives us that buzz, learning will be a joy.

Sure, you'll need to manage the weaker areas, but what if it was just that – managing them, rather than having to work on them over and over? I am not good at technical work, so I have someone in my team who helps me with it. I spend my life writing presentations, but it takes me ages to make anything look half-decent visually. I write notes of what I want and send it to a colleague who can impress me with something in minutes.

In other areas, I have to had to develop the skill myself, as we can't always rely on others to cover our gaps. I am not naturally a structured, organised person, and that just can't work with the volume of clients, projects and deadlines I have. I have found processes I can follow so I can work in a more organised way and ensure I always hit the deadlines.

I have managed my weaknesses rather than obsessing over needing to constantly improve them.

What are your strengths? How could you build on those and take them further? There is no limit to how far you could go.

It's worth highlighting that if you've had feedback that you're good at something, and you have said something like, "Oh no, everyone can do that!" then that is probably one of your strengths. Those things that are so simple to you, you can't imagine anyone else finding them difficult? Other people do find them difficult. This is your strength and when you acknowledge that, it could give you more confidence (feel-good bonus) and help you consider even better ways to use that strength.

What are your gaps or areas to develop? How could you cover the gaps? Or develop where you need to? Remember, you don't need to become the world's expert in your development area; that would be a waste of your energy. Aim for that with your strengths, whereas with your development areas, aim for them to be good enough – no longer having a negative impact on your work.

Let's look at how you might get a better, more objective view of how you're doing and then identify specific steps to become even more competent.

Benchmark

Do you have something you can use to track what is expected of you and how you're doing? I'd suggest a job description, but I know that many people don't have any paperwork that reflects their actual day-to-day work.

Maybe you've got objectives that were agreed at the start of the year? Or metrics that are important for your role? Look for a way of objectively benchmarking your performance.

It's not always easy to get a hard number for this, unless you work in sales and manufacturing: how much did you sell? How many did you make?

That doesn't mean we can't measure our progress. For someone to have had the finance department approve your role and salary, there must be a considered impact of your role. A considered value. What is that? Can you find out how your role is expected to impact the business and see about measuring that? Even if the measure is asking people.

Take being a manager as an example. Your performance is measured by the results of your team and, usually, an employee engagement survey. That survey is just asking someone else, on a scale of 1-5, how well they think you are doing your job. If you don't have such a survey in place, then it could be worth you asking people on a scale of 1-5 (or 1-4 if you're like me and want to avoid a load of middle scores), which leads us on beautifully to feedback.

Feedback

At the start of this chapter, I commented on our tendency to be too reliant on other people's views or, more likely, our perception of their views. We're so often obsessing about what we *think* other people think about us. What if instead we asked for feedback so that we *know* what people think about us? Then we could use that feedback to contribute to the broader picture we're building here of our skills and how we add value to the team.

Speaking to your colleagues and particularly your manager can be helpful. Ask: "How would you know if I was good at my job? What would you see and hear that would tell you I was doing well?" Often this ends up being about them, for example, "I'd have less checking to do" and "People would not come to me with process problems, because you had already resolved them."

A major issue we face in the workplace is that people are not very good at giving feedback. This makes gathering useful insights about our work rather challenging. The issues I see when managers and peers are struggling to give feedback boil down to a fear of causing offence and a lack of specificity. Which means either you get vague feedback in the hope that you don't feel upset, or you get vague feedback because the feedback provider just can't tell you what you did and what needs improving.

Here's how you could help others give you more useful feedback:

1. Ask for specifics. Instead of just saying to a colleague, "Can you give me some feedback please?" which could result in them saying you're a nice person or that you sometimes talk with your mouth full of food and it's annoying... ask for specifics. "I'm working on my project management skills, and I'd love your feedback on what I do well on our projects and what I could improve." You have explained what you're looking for and given parameters to the feedback you want, which is very useful in helping the other person give you specifics. Based on what they say, you could then ask for more specifics. For example, "Okay, so you find that when I lead project meetings, the meetings feel rushed and unstructured. Could you tell me more about that? Any examples you could share with me, so I can understand how I can improve?" An alternative or an add-on would be, "That's really useful feedback, thank you. Any ideas on how I could improve that? What do I need to do differently?"

2. Ask someone else. If I ask you for feedback and you give me something vague like "You can come across as unprepared," that might feel like the end of the conversation. But then I could go to someone else and start with a specific question. Instead of asking this second person for feedback, I can say, "I've heard that I can come across as unprepared, and I'd love to know when you've seen that and what I could do to improve. When have you seen me come across as unprepared?" Notice how with this wording you have not left room for the simple retort of "No, I don't think that of you at all!" That's purposeful, to encourage this second person to give you specifics.

3. Ask for in-the-moment feedback. When I have pushed for specifics and not gained any useful insights, a helpful alternative has been to say, "Could you tell me next time I do it? If we're in a meeting together and I come across as XYZ, could you wave at me or make a note of it to tell me about it later? I'd really appreciate that, as it will help me better understand what I'm doing and where I can improve."

It could be an addition into your thinking process to challenge the importance of others' views, and to invest time in finding people who can better support you through more specific and useful feedback.

Unspoken feedback

What are the signs you're doing well, without someone actually saying so? For example, for me as an external consultant, being invited back for more work, or being recommended to a client's friend in another business, that's a big sign I'm doing something right. It means a lot to me as well that when a contact at one client company moves employer, they take me with them to the new business.

How about for you? What are the unspoken signs that people appreciate you?

Being invited onto more projects? Being invited into meetings? Being asked for your opinion? What are other people doing and saying that suggests they value you?

Which, of course, can have negative implications too. If you're being invited onto every project and into every meeting, you'll need to start saying no at some point! But in terms of giving you an idea that people appreciate your input, it's a more objective indicator than relying on your own sense of self and confidence.

Usage

People might tell you your ideas are good, or that your projects have been successful, but do you see your outputs being used? And can you put any measures of success to those projects? Can you evaluate how well they delivered on the objectives? This is surely the most objective measure of success.

You may need to do some work to find this out, as it's not always obvious. Many businesses do not prioritise project or case reviews, as the more important and urgent thing is to dive into the next thing, so we rarely see the ripple effects of our work. It's worth asking a few questions to find out what is being used and how. What about going to one of your stakeholders and asking, "That project we worked on last year, what has happened with that? What impact did it have?"

I have a tendency of saying at the end of workshops that "…interesting isn't good enough. Interesting is a waste of your time." If I am coming to the close of a workshop, no matter what the content was, I push people to do something with the ideas we have discussed. If they do not use the ideas, but say it was all very interesting, then it has been a waste of their time.

The best feedback I received on this book in draft stage was that people had used the ideas. Put something into practice straight away.

Who could you go to and ask about how your ideas or work has been used, and the effects of that? This could give you a better measure of how you are doing than anything else.

What are your specific knowledge gaps?

We tell ourselves, "I don't know enough," which is unhelpful because it makes us feel we are not good enough. And there is no call to action to help us improve. Make that more specific by considering where you need to build knowledge and identify how you can do it.

I was working with a charity recently where a new manager was leading on fundraising applications. "I don't know enough," he told me, "to tell the story of how amazing this charity is and inspire the grant providers to want to get involved." The next step was clear. Instead of staring at his computer hoping to magically have that information and do a better job of fundraising, he got on the phone to two of the founding trustees and had 15 minutes with each of them. He heard about how they started, the pain, the challenges, the inspiration that kept them going.

A knowledge gap doesn't mean we need to study for years. Think about what specific questions you could ask someone, or search online or find a book on, to build the knowledge that will help you.

What are your specific skills gaps?

Just like knowledge, it is helpful for us to know exactly what we need to work on, and then work on it. Rather than just telling ourselves we are not good enough at something, we need to get specific and identify ways to build our abilities.

What tells you that you need to build your skill? What feedback or insight have you had about the gap between where you are now and where you need to be?

Penny was running her first strategic workshop; the stakes were high, and she thought it was going okay. Until a senior leader came to her in the break and told her it was not going well, and if Penny didn't change things, the leader was going to leave. Penny chose in that moment to ask, "How can I make this better?" And from there, she chose to observe great facilitators and see what they did. Penny learnt, practised, studied more and became an expert in her field – so much so that now she has written a book on the subject! I recommend it: Dr Penny Pullan – *Making Workshops Work*.

A caution at this point: don't get lost in study.

Remember those wise words about riding a bike from the Being Brave chapter (page 65)? If you want to ride a bike, sitting at home reading the manuals is not the best way to go about it.

Once you have identified what skills you need to develop, using feedback, self-reflection on your job profile, looking at what you find difficult etc., you need to plan out how to develop those skills.

And the best way to develop skills is to practise. To do the thing you want to get better at.

Reading about it, going on training, watching a YouTube video – these things might give you a few ideas, but then you need to go and do something with those ideas. You need to ride the bike, so to speak. Try something out, give it a go, see what actually works for you.

We also tend to learn more from people around us than we

do from books and how-to videos.

When I wanted to build my presentation skills and have a stronger impact with senior clients, I thought about the people I knew. Who did I know that was good at it? I started observing people and noticing what I liked, what I didn't and what seemed to have most impact. I asked a few people to chat with me about how they did the very thing that I had observed as highly effective.

After three conversations, I had picked up enough practical tips to have a go. To give a presentation trying out a few new ideas and see what worked for me.

As with trying anything new, it felt weird. I wondered if I looked a bit strange as I stumbled my way through. That's why it is critical that we try things out a few times, rather than write a new idea off first-go, because it didn't come across like I was totally comfortable with it. How then can we ever get comfortable with anything new?

How about setting yourself a goal of speaking to one person and reading one article online, then having a go at trying something new, all within a week? Review how it went using the earlier tips on measuring success, like feedback and usage. As you keep practising, those weird, uncomfortable new ideas will become natural habits you no longer notice.

Summary & Reflection

Being Competent is better than confidence because it's about being brilliant, not just feeling brilliant. And as a side benefit, when you can objectively see your success, you're likely to feel pretty good about yourself too.

Identifying ways to get better at what you do focuses you on action. Getting an objective view is critical to this because it's fact over feeling. Forget feeling like you're good at something and focus instead on finding out how good you really are. From there, you can identify your strengths to build on and know your areas for development, to decide what you want to do about them.

You might also find it helpful to do this reflection as though you are considering someone else's work. That can reduce the impact of any hang-ups of self-promotion, or an unhelpful modesty that stops you from talking about your strengths.

What have you achieved in your work?

_____

_____

_____

_____

_____

_____

_____

_____

_____

How have others responded to your work?

_____

_____

_____

_____

_____

_____

What have been the outcomes of the projects you have worked on?

_____

_____

_____

_____

_____

_____

_____

What happened afterwards? What was the usage or longer-term response to your work?

_____

_____

_____

_____

_____

_____

_____

_____

What feedback have you received – spoken and unspoken?

_____

_____

_____

_____

_____

_____

_____

_____

What does all this indicate about what you are good at? Could you summarise this into 1-3 strengths?

_____

_____

_____

_____

_____

How could you take those strengths even further? What could you do to get even better at these things?

_____

_____

_____

_____

_____

What does all this indicate about what you are not so good at? Could you summarise this into 1-3 gaps?

_____

_____

_____

_____

_____

Plan out how you can build your priority knowledge and skills.

Include different ways you can learn – observing people, asking them how they do it, reading, searching online.

Do something – get out and give your new ideas a go. Accept it will feel clunky first time. Give it a go again and see what works for you.

12

(Better than confidence is...)

Being Credible

Our final chapter in this Thinking Tools section is about ensuring other people have confidence in us. When it comes to influencing someone or getting an outcome you want from a manager, customer or stakeholder, you will need them to have confidence in you – regardless of how much confidence you have in yourself.

Being Credible is better than confidence because it directly affects your ability to influence. Whether you feel confident or not, you can still come across as credible, build trust and have others believe in you.

Do I believe you when you speak? Do I believe you are worth listening to?

Our brain is an incredibly complex, amazing structure that achieves unbelievable things.

Yet in some ways, it is also very lazy. It takes shortcuts and makes quick decisions, based on limited and even inaccurate information. I get it: if I were a complex structure responsible for survival, movement, emotional connection, memory – the list goes on and on of what the brain does – I may also be tempted to take some shortcuts.

Sadly, one of these shortcuts is about confidence. If we see someone speaking with confidence or putting forward an idea with an air of authority, we assume a level of competence too. We assume the idea must be good, because that person shared it with such confidence. What they are saying must be right, as they had no doubt in the way they said it.

Have you ever been on an interview panel? We can't help but be wowed by a candidate with a confident posture and clear communication. Yet when we read our interview notes afterwards, often we realise it was all style and no substance.

I am not an advocate of faking it. If you don't know your stuff, say so. But if you have read the previous chapters and are working on Being Outcome-Focused, Others-Focused and Competent, then you're going to be good. You're going to know what your skills are and where you have gaps. And that means you can put yourself across with genuine credibility, rather than style over substance.

Your challenge might be in knowing how to come across with credibility. How do you show other people that you know your stuff, particularly when you lack confidence?

Having run impact, influencing and presentation skills training and coaching for over a decade, the one thing I notice that always surprises people is that it is such small changes in behaviour that make the difference.

Let's have a look at the ways you can demonstrate your competence and have others believe in you, for meetings, presentations, interviews and general day-to-day life.

Pace and tone

The difference between someone coming across as credible in their field versus not knowing what they're talking about can be the pace of their speech. Do they seem calm and in control? Or panicked, as though they just want this over, because maybe they don't know what else to say?

It can be their tone: do they flick their tone up at the end of each sentence, making it sound like a question? As though they are perhaps not sure what they are saying is true, and want you to tell them "Yes, that's right, I agree with you"?

Think of someone you believe is a credible speaker, someone who you stop to listen to when they speak up in meetings. Pay attention to them next time you're with them. What are they doing? How are they speaking?

Most of the people I meet who worry about not coming across confidently in presentations think the key to success is preparation. I agree with this, yet most of us are not preparing in ways that are most helpful.

Yes, it is good to prepare your content: *what* you want to say. Then you must also consider *how* you want to say it.

Maybe not the whole thing... I was working with school teachers recently in a communication skills workshop, and it would be ridiculous for them to rehearse everything they want to say each day! Rehearsing how you want to start and how you want to finish can make a huge difference, not least because those are the bits of what you say that the audience will most likely remember. We often forget a lot of the meat in the middle and recall only the first impression and the final summary – so make those count.

Once you have done that preparation to sound more credible in your content, now work on your style. Practise saying your first few sentences and pay attention to your tone and pace. And this is not about finding the *right* tone and the *right* pace; in fact, the key is variety.

Maybe you start with a low tone, sounding serious, and speak in a slow pace as you introduce your topic. Then you build up, getting a little quicker as you raise an important question, and going higher in pitch because you're excited by it. Then pause. Give your audience time to process what you just said.

Variety is key because we get bored. If you listen to someone speak with the same tone of voice and same pace for a few minutes, you'll start to zone out. Their speech becomes background noise as you lose focus. And you don't want your key stakeholder or audience zoning out when you want to influence them!

But how do you get that variety? How do you do it in a way that seems natural? It's all about matching your tone and pace to what you are saying. If you're talking about something worrying, slow down and take a lower pitch, your seriousness echoed in your tone. If you're talking about something more exciting, even if it's just the projections that numbers could improve in the next quarter, show that hope and optimism in your tone of voice. And maybe you speed up just a touch as well, in anticipation of this future. Introduce pauses as you go, so that people have time to process what you're saying.

It is much easier to demonstrate this on video than to write about it in a book, so have a look at helenfrewin.com to see YouTube clips of me covering this in detail.

Humility

One of the most underrated leadership characteristics and human traits is humility. When we think about influencing someone and being credible, we tend to think of forthright, loud people demanding what they want. This is a big problem in itself, because we may think, "I don't want to be like that, so instead I'll say nothing."

Being credible includes being honest about what you don't know. It includes listening and respecting others. And that's because it shows you have nothing to prove.

How do you respond when someone's idea is better than yours? What do you say when someone listens to your idea and suggests a way to make it even better? Humility listens, is grateful, is open to making things better. Humility is a lack of self-importance and a belief that others are important too. You can demonstrate that by listening more intently and then saying something that *shows* you were listening.

Designing a Global Talent Programme for a top leisure brand was an interesting test of my humility. At every turn, a new stakeholder had an idea of how we could design the programme in a better way. I would make some tweaks, and then a new stakeholder would have an opposing view. Then a new country would get involved and say they needed something totally different. We've all had an experience like that, and it can be tough to stay humble. We might feel that every conversation is another knock to our confidence (and patience!) and that people should just accept what we're saying as right.

Listening, reflecting back what I was hearing and asking questions were my most valuable tools. "Okay, so this aspect of the programme won't work in your business because of X, is that right?" Plenty of nodding from my audience tells me I have understood correctly. "So, we need to find a way of adapting the programme so you can do Y. And given that other markets need the programme to do Z, what are your thoughts on how we can make this work?"

Whether you feel confident or not, demonstrating humility in this way will build trust and show that you are credible.

Asking questions that show you don't claim to have all the answers and you want to shape a solution *with* others helps key stakeholders feel included and valued.

Say something

The last critical piece we need to cover here is speaking up. You cannot influence, demonstrate your credibility or show others your potential by staying silent.

Many of us hope and expect that our hard work should speak for itself. Other people should just see how good I am based on my work. Sadly, it's not the case – particularly if we're talking about someone other than your direct manager. A more senior leader will generally not even know what work you have done unless you tell them about it.

Given that this is so important, in the next section we have a whole chapter dedicated to this: speaking up in meetings.

Summary & Reflection

Being Credible is better than confidence because you will be judged more on how you come across than on how you feel. People cannot see how you feel. By demonstrating your competence and therefore building trust you can ensure that others believe in you and want to listen to your ideas.

Think about a few people that you like to listen to. You trust what they say in presentations, and you would describe them as coming across with credibility and authority. They might be people in the public eye or someone you work with. Either way, take some time to observe them and reflect on what it is they do. How are they speaking? How are they standing or sitting? How do they vary their tone and pace as they speak?

Have a look at the Credibility and Impact videos on helenfrewin.com. What tips do you pick up here that you want to capture for your next presentation or meeting?

_____

_____

_____

_____

_____

_____

_____

What will you do in your next meeting or presentation to come across as more credible?

_____

_____

_____

_____

_____

_____

_____

_____

13

Building Your Toolkit

You have read seven chapters, seven tools, seven ways of challenging your thinking, to help you get better results. Confidence might make you feel good, but these little treasures will have you achieving far greater outcomes.

If you haven't already made use of the reflection questions, how about going back through the chapters you found most useful and doing that now?

It's what will change this book from being just a book to being your coach, your shift in perspective and your step towards your definition of success.

If you're looking for more guidance on *how* to use these tools, you'll appreciate Part 3. Here I've laid out the most common scenarios to show you how to apply the ideas in practice.

And if you'd like a summary on one page of all the best questions from each of the seven tools, well, you probably need to make your own. There will be different questions that strike each reader as most powerful. But if it's helpful, here are my top picks all on one page...

My top picks: questions from the thinking tools

What outcome do you want?

How would you know you had achieved it?

What if this wasn't about you? Who could this be for? What do they need?

How could you add value?

What are your specific fears about this?

If each fear became a reality, what could you do?

If you decided to be brave and take a first step, what could that be?

How can you get a more objective sense of how competent you are?

What do you need to do to become even better?

When it comes to communicating and influencing, how could you have more credibility?

*I love thinking about the power of purpose...
because it shifts our gaze from how we're acting
and appearing towards what we most deeply
want to be and do and support.*

And where our gaze goes, we go.

Deborah Henson-Conant

PART 3

Success in Practice

14

Overview

When I first decided to write a book about thinking tools that are better than confidence, it did strike me this was a bit strange. Confidence and Imposter Syndrome workshops make up about 5% of my work. This is not my bread and butter.

People management, leadership development, executive coaching, interview skills, personal effectiveness, relationship-building, business partnering and consulting skills – these are the subjects I spend most of my time on.

In every single one of those topics, be it a year-long programme or one-off workshop, confidence comes up as a challenge.

Confidence, or at least coping with a lack of it, *is* therefore my bread and butter. It is an underlying theme in everything I do.

In the previous section, I outlined thinking tools that are

useful for any context. What I know from my work is that people need context. It's no good for me to just say, "Use these tools for anything," because then we're not sure when and how to use them.

It is for this reason that I have written Part 3 – to give you specific examples of how and when you could use these tools. To give more stories and add practical tips from the workshops I run all the time.

If you want to go straight to a situation you're facing, so you can read up on the tools that can help you today, here's where you can find each context:

Speaking up in meetings – chapter 15, page 137

Presentations – chapter 16, page 151

Difficult conversations – chapter 17, page 159

Going for a promotion/new job/pay rise – chapter 18, page 173

Receiving feedback – chapter 19, page 185

It's worth remembering that this is not meant to be a guide on how to give a presentation or how to get your dream job. Each of those is a book in itself.

This is a guide to get you to the starting line. If you think you need more confidence in these situations, these chapters show you how to use the Better Than Confidence Thinking

Tools. How you then proceed is up to you.

That said, I couldn't help myself... I have added a few tips along the way that will help you get better outcomes. Enjoy!

15

Speaking Up in Meetings

I have started with this one because it is the first question that is raised in workshops on imposter syndrome. And it comes up a lot in career coaching and accelerator programmes for underrepresented groups. Then you've got the leadership development workshops, where delegates raise that they're fine with their direct reports, but when in meetings with peers and senior leaders, they are not confident to speak up.

We get that promotion, or we get invited onto a project, and we feel like we need to add value by speaking up in meetings. But can I add any value? Other people know more than I do. What if I say something stupid or suggest an idea that won't work?

Ayman joined an Imposter Syndrome workshop at a retail client, as he was on a project team that he felt unsure about. He had been invited onto that project because of his track record in implementing new technology in his own store. But what did he know about convincing other managers to try out new kit?! How could he possibly convince business managers to invest in technology? This was not his skillset. He knew the project would be good for his career, because it was high profile and it took him out of his store, helping towards a head office or area management role. But Ayman felt completely out of his depth and had no idea what to say in the meetings.

For Ayman, and hundreds more like him, the following were the tools that had the biggest impact. Better than waiting for confidence, these steps helped him take immediate action.

What outcome do you want?

Ayman found it helpful to answer this in two ways – firstly for him personally, he wanted people to think he was credible and that he added a lot of value to the project, so he was in a better position for future promotion opportunities. Secondly, he wanted the project to succeed, for more stores to invest in the new technology, so the whole business could improve. He felt passionately about that because of the difference he had seen the kit make to his business. This clarity helped him realise that if he did the latter piece of helping the business, then that would do him a lot of favours for his personal goals too.

What if it wasn't about you?

Ayman's thinking above led beautifully onto making it less about him. Instead of thinking about how to come across with credibility and impress senior leaders, he focused more on how he could add value. How could he convince other store managers of the benefits of this technology? What experiences could he share to help them? How could he help with implementation? Notice that difference – he has gone from thinking he has no skills or knowledge to offer, to thinking specifically about *how* he can help.

What do I know/what value can I add?

This was all linking together now for Ayman as he realised that his stories, his numbers, the problems he faced and how he had overcome them were exactly what other store managers would want to hear.

Kinga faced a similar situation to Ayman's, albeit in a completely different context of moving into a more senior role in her law firm and being expected to speak up in client meetings. I was coaching Kinga after she had gone through a Senior Associate Development Centre and she was unsure how she could speak up more. All these meetings were online, with a global client team dialling in from all around the world.

Kinga shared Ayman's concerns about what to say, plus she was also concerned about *how* to speak up, or how to interject. There was usually a lot of discussion from a lot of confident voices, with little pause for her to chime in. This meant that another question was needed:

What specific fears or concerns do you have about speaking up?

"I don't want to speak just for the sake of it," Kinga explained. "I hate it when people do that. People might think I just like the sound of my own voice.

Other people talk a lot, so I don't know how to interject, how to cut in – and it feels rude talking over other people. What if people think I'm rude and inappropriately interrupting?"

Working through the process in the Being Prepared chapter was incredibly useful, and Kinga found this opened up a lot of ideas for her.

What could you do to reduce the chances of people thinking you like the sound of your own voice? Hearing this question out loud, Kinga immediately let this one go – "Well, I'm not going to be speaking half as much as everyone else, so I don't think this is really an issue!"

Have you ever had that happen to you? You have a fear and then you realise that this fear is baseless, and you can immediately let it go? It is such a powerful moment. Releasing, a breath of fresh air, a pressure lifted.

Use these questions to help you get those moments more often.

What is your fear?

What could you do to reduce the chance of that happening?

And if it did happen, what would you do then?

When I asked Kinga, "What could you do to reduce the chances of people thinking you are rude and inappropriately interrupting?" she went silent. This one would need more thought.

Kinga needed a way of coming into the conversation. She wanted something to say at the start rather than just blurting her way in. "What if I say, 'Sorry can I just add...'?" she suggested. "It seems polite for me to do that."

In the past, I have been someone that encourages people to stop apologising. Stop diminishing the power of what you are saying. How often do you use phrases like:

"I don't know if this is a rubbish idea, but..."

"I know I'm not the expert in the room, but I wonder if...."

"Sorry to interrupt, is it worth us considering...."

These statements can reduce your authority and credibility. Better to just say what you want to say and avoid the fluff around the edges.

But now I wonder if I have been wrong about this.

Recently, I was running a confidence workshop for one of

the biggest brands in the world and we had a guest speaker: the Global Chief Operations Officer. He shared that he still says in many meetings, "I'm not the marketing expert, but..." and "I know I'm not the expert in the room on this, I just have a view that..."

Some of his colleagues over the years have told him to "be more confident." And he pushes back. He believes that confidence is not always helpful and that telling someone to be more confident is distracting and unhelpful advice. I like this guy.

He tells these colleagues, "It's a fact that I am not a marketing expert, and so it feels only appropriate to say that, then share my idea, and be open to others in the room who know more about it telling me I'm wrong or helping to build on my idea. It is a way of being inclusive and encouraging of others' views. When I ask people what they think and how we could do things better, I believe they will speak up more because I have pitched my expertise as lower than theirs. I believe this is better leadership."

I was blown away by his comments. Not only did I (obviously) agree with his points on confidence, but here he was role modelling vulnerability and great leadership by using self-deprecating statements.

That same week, as I was working with Kinga and other senior associates in the law firm, Kinga told me that without something to ease her in, like "Sorry, can I just add..." she could not imagine speaking up at all. We talked about other things she could say to interject, like, "From the project perspective..." or "Based on the project history, I suggest..." But these did not feel right for her.

Kinga explained that the simple fact was she would be interrupting. There was no space. On every occasion, she would be speaking over someone else. And the only way she could imagine doing that was to start with an apology.

Is it better for me to tell Kinga that she is wrong? Or is it better for Kinga to speak up in a way that feels right for her?

My conclusion: it is better for you to speak up with an apology and self-deprecating statements than not to speak up at all.

I still encourage you to move away from constant apologies and comments that reduce your credibility. But perhaps that can come with time. Maybe your first step in courage today is to speak up with the apology. And maybe in future you can drop the apology.

Which is exactly what happened for Kinga.

Once she got used to speaking up and noticed that nobody seemed bothered at all about her interrupting, it was only a couple of meetings before she dropped the apology. Now she contributes throughout meetings with ease and comfort.

As a final add-on, see if asking a different kind of 'what if...?' question could be useful for you, to overcome a lack of confidence about speaking up in meetings. Try out these questions and see if they shift anything in your thinking...

What if you believed you had as much right as anyone else to be heard in this meeting?

What if you believed that people appreciate you and want to hear what you have to say?

Summary & Reflection

What outcome do you want from speaking up more in meetings? You may find it useful to make specific notes about each meeting where you want to be contributing more.

_____

_____

_____

_____

_____

_____

_____

_____

What value could you add to those meetings?

_____

_____

_____

_____

_____

_____

_____

_____

What if it wasn't about you, but about helping others? Or improving the business in some way?

_____

_____

_____

_____

_____

_____

_____

What specific fears do you have about speaking up in that meeting? Work through the steps for each fear of 1) what could you do to reduce the chances of that fear becoming a reality? And 2) if the worst happened, and the fear did become reality, what could you do to respond?

_____

_____

_____

_____

_____

_____

_____

What is the cost of you not speaking up in that meeting?

_____

_____

_____

_____

_____

_____

_____

What if you believed you had every right to speak up?

What if you believed that people appreciate you and want to hear what you have to say?

_____

_____

_____

_____

_____

_____

_____

_____

_____

According to most studies, people's number one fear is public speaking. Number two is death. Death is number two. Does that seem right? That means to the average person, if you have to go to a funeral, you're better off in the casket than doing the eulogy.

Jerry Seinfeld

16

Presentations

I'm sure it won't surprise you that presentations are a joint first or close second to speaking up in meetings, in terms of self-belief challenges. At every workshop I run on confidence, impact or personal effectiveness, I get asked about presentations.

I need to present an idea or gain buy-in to my idea.

My manager wants me to present more, but I fall apart every time.

Now I'm in a more senior position I have to present to clients and colleagues weekly, but I always feel so anxious.

People tell me they need more confidence to be better presenters. They need to be positive thinkers. I of course challenge that idea and give them some thinking tools instead.

Being Outcome-Focused is always the best starting point. What outcome do you want from your presentation? What do you want people to do? To think? To feel?

When my colleague Krush started facilitating training years ago, she tells me, she used to watch one of her peers and say: "You went totally off topic. How have you still got to the point?!" It surprised her that a presentation or workshop discussion could achieve the same outcome, even if the journey to get there was very different. Krush's colleague explained that he always had the objective in mind: he knew where he needed to get to, and it didn't matter how he got there. This is the power of the outcome focus. It means we can focus less on saying a specific statement or following a set process as long as we keep a focus on where we want to get to.

This is a far more powerful starting point than, "What do I want to say?" I've had countless training sessions where people tell me the first thing they do when they prepare for a presentation is open PowerPoint and start creating slides. Disaster. In this case we're immediately focused on what to say, how to present, what visuals to use, and totally unaware of why we're doing this in the first place.

And that focus on what to say and how to present can lead to anxiety and us starting to panic that we don't know what we're doing. How can I know what to say when I haven't even got clarity on why I'm speaking?

By starting instead with the outcome you want, you can laser focus on that. Why is this outcome important? Who is the audience? What's important to them? Given what you know about your audience, what could help them get to the outcome you want? If you have been asked to present and you don't know the answers to these questions, then who could you ask? And if you can't get answers, could you make some educated guesses?

On a presentation skills workshop, Jendra told me she had no idea about her audience, so how could she prepare to get buy-in to her business proposal? I asked her to tell me what she did know about them, and what she could estimate based on that. "Well, it's the finance team," she started. Jendra smiled as she realised she could make a lot of reasonable assumptions about what they would need. "They'll want to know about budget, how my proposal affects profitability and I think they'll also want a long-term picture of why this is a good idea. I also imagine they might be risk-averse, so telling them what the risks are and how we can manage them could head off questions and concerns."

That last bit is crucial. How often do we panic about presentations because we worry about being asked a question we don't know the answer to? Or, worse, we worry about being asked *that particular question*, which we don't want to discuss.

Instead of simply panicking, or thinking we need more confidence, what if we focused on Being Prepared? Spend time thinking about what the audience might need, what questions they might have. And yes, preparing to answer that question we don't want as well. Then we will feel prepared and in control, so we are able to do our best in the presentation.

Whenever people in a workshop ask what they should do if they don't know the answer to a question, they seem unhappy with the response. Whether it's me or someone else in the room who comes up with the simple solution to, "Tell them you don't know," this is somehow unsatisfactory.

Do you share this concern? Maybe you think that it is not good enough to politely say, "Good question. I don't know, so I'll go and look into it and come back to you by the end of the day." If you think this is unacceptable as a response, then I encourage you to consider the Being Challenging chapter (page 89), as this could be perfectionism at play. You can't expect yourself (or anyone else) to know everything.

You might also benefit from the humility section of Being Credible (page 117), as admitting what you don't know can boost other people's confidence in what you do know.

On the humility note, it can be worth considering how you could make the presentation more interactive. Because it's called a presentation, we picture ourselves *presenting*, one-way. But what if that's not so helpful for achieving our outcome? Opening something up for discussion and showing that you value others' ideas and feedback can boost your impact. This is humility at play, and whether you feel confident or not, this makes you look more in control and like you have nothing to prove.

Body language is also something to consider here because this can be a cause for concern. We worry about not looking confident and in control. "What should I do with my hands?!" is a question I get asked in every presentation skills workshop.

The key is to look comfortable. At ease. How do you look when you're at ease? I drink a lot of water, and that also helps with me taking pauses during presentations, so I will often have a glass of water in my hand. At other times my hands are loosely together, so I can move into gesticulating naturally and easily. Watch other people and see what they do. Notice how you stand and move when you're feeling relaxed.

Read back over the Being Credible chapter (page 117) to help you prepare to look confident and speak with authority.

Summary & Reflection

Start with the outcome – what do you want the audience to do? Think? Feel? Why is that important to you?

_____

_____

_____

_____

_____

Who is your audience? What is important to them? What might be the connection between the outcome you want and what they want? If they often talk about profit, link your idea to profit. If they're always speaking about customers, talk about customers.

_____

_____

_____

_____

_____

_____

What questions or concerns do you think your audience might have? Is it even worth you sounding out one or two people to find out? How could you be prepared for those questions, or even cover them early on and ease concerns, e.g. "You might be wondering how this fits with X strategy; here's how…" and "If you're concerned about profit, I would be too given the spend I'm talking about. Here are the projections and how we can manage the risk…"

How could you make the presentation more interactive?

17

Difficult Conversations

How much confidence do you need to have a difficult conversation?

I mentioned earlier that I once worked with a business owner who had put off a difficult conversation for *fifteen years*. That's extreme, but I have also had delegates in every workshop on people management and honest conversations tell me they have put off saying something important.

Sometimes people tell me it is fear of the other person's reaction that stops them; others say it's that they just need more confidence. Either way, by the end of the workshop delegates are more focused on specific tools to prepare for and have a conversation.

In most cases, I find the aversion to difficult conversations comes down to the fear of the discomfort of the conversation *outweighing* the fear of not addressing the issue.

The benefit of having the conversation is not considered worth the perceived nastiness.

Yet we tend to make this decision without actually considering the cost of doing nothing. That will definitely be one of the useful questions from Being Prepared that we'll cover in this chapter.

What are you imagining is a difficult conversation? Here are some classics I hear:

I need to give someone in my team constructive feedback.

I want to challenge a colleague/someone more senior about their decision.

I want to challenge inappropriate behaviour from a colleague/friend/family member.

My partner and I disagree on something fundamental; I need to talk to them about it.

I'm worried about my child and don't know how to talk to them about it.

My elderly parents need more care, but they don't want to admit it.

In all cases, Being Outcome-Focused is once again the best starting point. What outcome do you want from the conversation? What do you want people to do? To think? To feel? What do you want to happen after this conversation? Or maybe it's a longer-term outcome, as we don't always (if ever) get what we want from just one conversation.

This is critical to realise: it may take more time than you hope to get the outcome you want. Aiming to completely turn around a poor performer in one conversation is somewhat unrealistic. It may take months of feedback and review. Convincing elderly parents that they need support could take even longer, as often pride and not wanting to be a burden are strong emotional drivers that get in the way of openness to change.

Confidence or unrealistic optimism could be unhelpful here if you expect everything to be fixed after one discussion.

What outcome do you want overall? And what outcome might be feasible to hope for after this first conversation? Maybe you simply want to make your parents aware that you are thinking about their long-term needs, and that you would like them to be thinking about that too. With your underperformer, giving them the specific feedback on what needs improving is a great starting point. That will probably do for the first conversation, and then you can review over time how well they have responded to the feedback and whether they are making improvements.

You may also need to challenge that desired outcome on occasion. Is the outcome what's best for the business? For others? Or just what's best for you?

It concerns me sometimes when I hear people say, "I want them to realise I'm right," or "I want them to go with my idea." Do we get so attached to being right or having the best idea that we lose focus on hearing others' ideas? Do we miss the opportunity to listen and understand the other person's thinking?

As a participant on a leadership development programme, Esme knew she was in a safe space to share some serious frustrations. Esme was extremely upset about a restructure that had changed her team from five people to two. She had explained to the managers involved that this would mean a reprioritising of work, which would lead to certain decreases in results. At the time, management nodded and agreed, but once those results actually dropped, it was a different story.

Esme had been asked to present to management on what had caused the problem and how she would resolve it. She knew this would be a difficult conversation and she kept getting stuck on her desired outcome. "I want them to realise that I told them this would happen – that this drop in numbers is the only option unless they give me more people. They need to realise they got this wrong."

Can you imagine the conversation? Not pleasant. Nobody in the management team is going to say, "Yes, you're right, Esme. Thanks for pointing out my stupidity."

Esme sounded confident and forthright in her views, but her thinking was not so helpful.

What if Esme focused on the common goals instead – to see

DIFFICULT CONVERSATIONS

results improve, for the business to do well, for the team to be thriving? Let's agree on what we're aiming for, the challenges we're facing and then explore together how we could overcome those challenges. It becomes a group brainstorm rather than a one-person mission to prove management wrong.

Once you're clear on the outcome you want and have sense-checked that it's good for others too, you can move on to addressing specific fears. What is it you worry about happening? The underperformer crying? Quitting? The more senior colleague getting angry, threatening to fire you? Your child getting upset and giving you the silent treatment for months?

Let's use the Being Prepared process here:

What is your fear? List out your specific worries of things that could go wrong.

For each one, what could you do to reduce the chance of that happening?

And if it did happen, what could you do then?

To bring balance to all that thinking, what is the cost to you of not having this conversation?

Now it's time for Being Brave and some "How can I do this?" planning. What is the first step you could take? Again, when you realise you will probably not get to your overall desired

163

outcome in one conversation, you can start thinking in smaller steps instead. Rather than going to the poor performer with, "If you don't change this behaviour, then in six months I'll be firing you," you can just start with feedback. One step with a senior colleague could be to sound out how open they are to challenge from you. I have personally had every point on the response spectrum hit with this one.

Marcus was a manager I didn't like and I struggled to understand. When I raised with him that I "wasn't sure" about a decision he had made – as an attempt to sound him out for me giving the more complete truth that I disagreed with him with every bone in my body – he asked me if I wanted to leave the company.

Okay, test complete: this is not a manager I can have an open conversation with. At this point I had a choice. Do I want to bite my tongue and carry on working here? Or is that not an option for me?

Back then, for various reasons, it was worth me sticking it out just a bit longer. But I knew I would be leaving soon, and that helped me cope.

At the other end of the scale, Carolyn was a manager I respected deeply, and she was struggling with a few things. When I suggested one small way she might improve, to test out the relationship, she was open and encouraging. Carolyn appreciated my view, valued my help and wanted to improve herself. I gave her more suggestions and challenged her when I could see things were not going well. We worked incredibly well together, and the trust simply grew and grew.

What is a small step you could take? If your conversation feels scary, is there a smaller conversation you could use to test the water? Based on how well that conversation goes, you can judge your next steps. We often feel more confident once we've started; even if it gets complicated, we at least know we're on the journey towards our desired outcome.

Don't get me wrong, I write all this about taking small steps, but sometimes we just need to rip the plaster off.

"I'm sorry to tell you this, but I know I would want to know if it was me. You smell bad."

"I need to make you aware we will not be renewing your contract."

If it's that simple, then rip off that plaster. Doing anything other than that will confuse the other person, waste your time and probably lead to you feeling even more awkward.

But in most cases, there are steps towards the outcome you want. Start identifying them.

Once you've taken a step, it's worth reflecting on what happened, what you learnt and what you might try differently next time. What works today with one person might not work next week, or with someone else, as we are all different. This means we need to be open to trying things out and finding what works.

Your confidence or more helpful thinking can come from the knowledge that there is no one right way to do this. Take the pressure off your shoulders that you need to have the conversation perfectly, as there is no such thing, and do the best you can.

It all comes back to the outcome and it being worth it. If the cost of doing nothing is not acceptable to you, then giving it your best shot is absolutely worth it.

Summary & Reflection

What outcome do you want overall? You might not get there in one conversation, but where do you want to get to?

_____

_____

_____

_____

_____

_____

_____

How does that outcome benefit you? The other person? The broader team/business/family? Use this question to sense-check that this isn't only good for you.

_____

_____

_____

_____

_____

_____

_____

Given that overall outcome, what might be a feasible outcome to aim for in this first conversation?

What do you want the person to do? Think? Feel? Say?

How could you go about getting to that first conversation outcome?

_____

_____

_____

_____

_____

_____

_____

_____

What are your fears? List your specific worries of things that could go wrong.

_____

_____

_____

_____

_____

_____

_____

_____

For each one, what could you do to reduce the chance of that happening?

And if it did happen, what could you do then?

To bring balance to all that thinking, what is the cost to you of not having this conversation?

_____

_____

_____

_____

_____

_____

_____

_____

_____

_____

_____

_____

_____

_____

_____

_____

_____

_____

_____

18

Going for a Promotion

I have used the word 'promotion' in this chapter heading, but the content is equally relevant to similar things like asking for a pay rise or applying for a new role in a new company.

We have seen in previous chapters how the brain's attempts at self-preservation makes us small. When we tell ourselves we cannot do XYZ, we might fail, we might be rejected... We stop. We choose not to try. And then the brain says to us, "See, I told you so. Because you followed my advice and did nothing, you are currently feeling okay. You are not feeling rejected, useless, embarrassed, a failure. You should always listen to me. I will protect you from harm."

It is often this line of unconfident thinking that stops us from applying for that job or asking for the pay rise we believe we have been owed for some time.

The thing is, what is the cost of that protection? It's never stepping out and discovering what we could become; not getting the money we have earned.

And what if failure and rejection aren't so bad anyway?

Overcoming a lack of confidence to go for what you want starts with a good understanding of what you want. Yes, we're back to Being Outcome-Focused.

What are you looking for? There are more questions in the Summary and Reflection section on page 180 to help you explore this.

If you want to ask for a pay rise, this may well be about fairness. I hear far too many stories of people who were asked to 'act up' into a role and three years later they're still not being paid to deliver that role. Or a classic I heard the other day from my friend Lily: "A colleague quit because he could not handle the workload of a role. The responsibilities were too complex and there were too many of them, and he had raised this for a while. When nothing changed, he left and found a job elsewhere.

"What did the company do in response? Split that role in two? Reorganise how that work was delivered? No. That large complex role that was too much for one person got added on to someone else's workload! And do you think that person got offered extra money to take on all that? Of course not." As employers, sometimes we treat our people so badly it pains me.

So, fight it! If you are in a position like that, you need to fight for what is fair, for what is right. If you're doing the job, shouldn't you be paid to do that job? If you're 'acting up' to see if you can deliver what's required, that's fine in principle; just make sure there are clear timescales and success measures agreed, otherwise you could find yourself in the same position more than a year later.

Worrying that this all sounds selfish? You may well be familiar with the gender pay gap and the trend that men usually negotiate for better salaries than women. As with all gender differences, it's worth highlighting that this is about macro-trends: there are plenty of women who negotiate hard and plenty of men who would never ask for a pay rise. Yet on every programme I am asked to run, call it a Women's Leadership Development Programme or a Breaking the Glass Ceiling Programme for all underrepresented groups at exec levels, selfishness and fear are given as reasons to not ask for a pay rise or step up for promotions and opportunities.

Is it selfish for you to be paid fairly, so you can provide for your family? Is it selfish for you to be recognised for what you do, so you are more likely to stay with the company and have them benefit from your skills? Isn't it in the company's interest to ensure you feel you are paid fairly and acknowledged for the value you add? If it was your manager's choice to do that or lose you, which do you think they would choose?

This is starting to use the Being Others-Focused ideas of considering who else this is for or who else benefits.

"What advice would you give to someone else?" is an incredibly powerful question here, because it pulls us out of our own heads. Instead of worrying about being selfish, or being seen to be selfish, imagine someone else had this issue. Your best friend, your niece, that colleague you have taken under your wing and want to see succeed... What if they came to you with the idea that they maybe wanted to ask for a pay rise or a promotion, but they were worried about... (fill in your own concerns). What advice would you give them?

Follow that with the Being Prepared questions and working through your specific fears. Classic fears I hear in this area are:

What if my manager says I don't deserve a pay rise?

What if I go through the pain of asking for what I want, and I don't get it?

What if I get the promotion and fail?

Whatever your concerns and fears, work through them, considering what you could do to avoid that becoming the reality and what you would do if it did happen. Then ask that great question: what is the cost of doing nothing?

The Being Challenging chapter on page 89 could be a useful read for you as well, to explore any fear of failure that could be holding you back.

When it comes to self-promotion, many of us struggle with putting across our abilities and achievements out of a fear of failure or rejection.

What if I say I can do X and my manager says I'm wrong, they don't think I'm so good?

What if I sound like I'm arrogant and they don't like me?

Spend time exploring what is at the heart of your discomfort. If it's a fear like these, then again, work through the fear. How could you reduce the chance of coming across as arrogant, yet still show what you can do?

Sometimes confidence is not the issue at all. I have discovered that there are plenty of people who have the confidence to go for what they want, but it turns out some of them need something better than confidence. They need to know *how* to sell themselves. I first learnt this with Katharine.

Katharine had been applying to medical schools for a while and getting nowhere. Her grades were great, but she'd had countless interviews, all resulting in rejection. A mutual friend suggested I might be able to help, so he introduced us. I met with Katharine and asked her about her experience and what made her think she would make a good doctor.

As Katharine talked, my heart sank. It seemed like she had no useful experience or skills. I'm never going to push someone to lie, sell themselves and get a job they can't do and shouldn't be applying for. That would go against everything I believe in. So I felt bad for Katharine that I was about to crush her dreams. I could see why she had not been successful, and I wanted to explain it to her as clearly and helpfully as possible.

But then.

Wow.

In one last attempt to see if there was anything there, I asked Katharine to tell me a story. "Tell me about something that happened that made you think you wanted to be a doctor."

A different person started talking. A person full of compassion and proactivity. Someone willing to get involved, someone watching out for opportunities, someone who had studied enough to be able to help in a challenging situation, years before any official training.

Wow. I told her what I had been thinking and how this story changed everything. I asked her to tell me more stories like that and out they flowed.

Katharine had everything she needed; she just didn't know how to communicate this to the interviewers. We talked about which stories she could share, for which sorts of interview questions, and we explored the outcome question from the other angle. "What outcome do you think the medical school interviewers are looking for? What do you think they want to see in you?"

I was not surprised when Katharine received offers from every single medical school she applied to after that. Whilst I was over the moon for Katharine, this experience also had a profound impact on me. I started wondering how many more people were out there like Katharine. People with all the potential and drive that the world needs, who don't know how to say things in the 'right' way for that potential to be recognised.

Confidence was not the issue for Katharine, though there is no doubt it had taken a huge knock from all the rejections. More confidence might have felt good, but Katharine needed something better. She needed clarity on what the interviewers were looking for, what skills and experience she had and how to connect those dots in the interview. My hope is that this book is a help to more people in that situation.

Reflect on the Being Others-Focused chapter (page 53) questions when you are preparing for an interview and potentially even asking for a pay rise, as it will help you prepare.

What do you think the interviewer wants out of this? What do they want to know? How can you reassure them? What story can you share to demonstrate what you can do?

Summary & Reflection

If you never ask and never apply, you'll never get what you want. So, isn't it better to give it a go?

Don't let a lack of confidence stop you from Being Brave and trying something new.

When you think about this job/promotion/pay rise, what outcome do you want? What is important to you about that? And why is that important to you?

_____

_____

_____

_____

_____

_____

_____

_____

_____

_____

_____

_____

_____

What do you believe the new job/promotion/pay rise will give you? Is it just about more money? Status? Are you attracted to working for a different company or doing a different role? Take your thinking further to clarify more about what you want. This could help you reality-check your expectations. I say this because I have had countless people over the years tell me that they went for the people management promotion for status and more money but then they hated managing a team!

What are your specific fears? List your worries of things that could go wrong.

_____

_____

_____

_____

_____

_____

_____

_____

For each one, what could you do to reduce the chance of that happening?

_____

_____

_____

_____

_____

_____

_____

_____

And if it did happen, what could you do then?

_____

_____

_____

_____

_____

_____

_____

_____

_____

To bring balance to all that thinking, what is the cost to you of not applying/asking?

_____

_____

_____

_____

_____

_____

_____

_____

If you're asking for a pay rise, what might be in it for the person you're asking? To keep you in the business? To keep you feeling valued and doing your best? This is not about threatening that you will quit (unless you actually will), it's about highlighting that it is in the business' interest as well to keep you feeling good about working there.

If you're applying for a job, what might the interviewers be looking for? How can you demonstrate to them that you can match that? What stories can you tell about when you have shown the skills they're looking for?

19

Receiving Feedback

Why have I included a chapter on receiving feedback in this book?

Maybe you could understand the need for confidence, or something better than confidence, to *give* feedback. But to *receive* feedback? What's that got to do with confidence or getting the outcomes we want in life?

The way you ask for, receive, and respond to feedback can make a huge difference in your relationships and in your ability to develop yourself, not to mention your career prospects. And I meet people every day who lack the confidence to ask for feedback. They fear being told they are not good enough.

This could be the big annual appraisal or a scary career conversation like, "Do you think I have the potential to be a director here?" More everyday feedback like, "How did that meeting go?" and "Were you happy with my contribution to this project?" can be just as fear-inducing.

And it's important to note that this fear is not relative to your competence. People who are brilliant at their jobs can fear feedback just as much as a poor performer.

We avoid asking for feedback because we lack the confidence or useful thinking to be able to handle it.

And that avoidance of feedback could be getting in the way of you achieving your goals. If you want to develop your career, run a business or be successful in anything, you will need to hear from others about how you can improve.

That's why I have included this chapter. To help you overcome a lack of confidence or unhelpful beliefs about feedback. Then you can ask for more feedback and be all the better for it.

What exactly are we afraid of?

Let's start with getting clear on what you fear when it comes to feedback.

Fear of not being good enough – as though a piece of work going wrong is tied to your identity. It's not something you did that you could learn from and improve, it is in your bones. You are not enough.

Fear of rejection – as though your manager telling you that this project did not go well is a personal attack and their way of saying "I don't want you in my team anymore. Nobody wants you."

Have a read of the Being Challenging chapter on page 89 if you'd like to think differently about failure and perfectionism, as that can help with releasing yourself from these fears. Better things to be believing are:

I can be a good person and get it wrong.

I can be worthy of friendship, love and affection and at times do a terrible job.

Have you ever worried about not being liked? Most of us have! When I discovered that a friend's new girlfriend didn't like me, I was mortified. What was wrong with me?! Why didn't she like me? What did I do wrong?

Early on in my career, my bonus was linked to my scores on workshop evaluations, often referred to as 'happy sheets'. You know when you go on training and you fill in a form at the end to say you thought the trainer was okay, the bacon sandwiches could have been warmer, and you didn't like the carpet? That's the one.

There was a question on our happy sheets that said, "On a scale of 1-10, how likely are you to recommend this facilitator?"

Anything less than a 10 felt like a knife wound.

It was personal, it was about my identity, my likeability; if it was less than a 10 then they didn't like me.

On my journey to becoming a better presenter, a mentor made me realise that this obsession with worrying about what other people think is pointless. We are all judging each other all the time. We are deciding in each moment what we like about someone, what we don't like. And all that is incredibly subjective and mostly out of our control.

I can do my best, be my best. And if you don't like me, then that's that. Not much else I can do. If you give me specific feedback on what I need to improve, I can work on it. But if you just don't like me? Not much I can do. So let it go.

What if you could let it go?

Now I'm going to ask for your openness and forgiveness for this one, because I know some people hate this phrase. What if you believed feedback was a gift? What if you believed feedback was one of the best ways you could grow and improve?

Would you like to be better at your job next year than you are today?

Would you like to have stronger relationships next year than you do today?

If you believe feedback is a way to get there, then feedback is indeed a gift.

When I let go of the need to be liked, I accepted that anything less than a 10 on a happy sheet was not a personal attack. I considered there might be something I could learn. Everything shifted.

Instead of being upset by a 9 or a 4 on the scale, I could look for more information. If I knew who wrote it, I could even ask them, "How could I improve?" and "What would have made it a 10?"

And.

Now this is a big one.

I also have the choice to not take that feedback on board.

Before my revelation that worrying about what people think is pretty pointless, when I was still highly sensitive to feedback, I had this experience: "You come across as patronising, Helen," I was told after a leadership meeting.

Whilst I felt like I was dying inside, I managed to find some useful words…

"Oh. That's not good. Can you tell me what I said or did that was patronising? I definitely want to improve that."

"It's just the way you are," my colleague replied.

Do you remember me commenting earlier that some (if not most) people are just not good at giving feedback? Case in point. What am I supposed to do with that?!

With no other feedback or information to support this, it

may have been better for me to let this go. To not take the feedback on board. We have that choice when feedback is not clear or helpful.

But as chance would have it, Linda came to save the day. I am so grateful that my colleague Linda was in earshot of this conversation. She approached me later and gave me her view. "You ask people difficult questions. Questions they don't have answers to. I know you're asking the questions to get them to think. To help them explore. But because they're insecure and feel under pressure to have the right answer, they call you patronising. They feel like you're trying to catch them out and make them look stupid."

What a difference! Now I had something solid to work with, I focused on framing my questions at the start of meetings. I explained why I was asking questions and where I was aiming for us to get to. It transformed my conversations.

I could have chosen to not take the feedback on board, because there was nothing I could work with, and I wondered if it was just a comment from a disgruntled colleague. But with Linda's add-ons, I could learn, grow, transform.

Responding

When people tell me they lack the confidence to ask for feedback, this is often followed by the question, "...and how should I respond to it?"

Whilst feedback can sting, as with most things in life it's not what happens that matters most, it's how you react. Or, better, because *react* sounds instant and not thought-through, how you choose to *respond*.

It's worth being ready. It's worth having a prepared response and useful thinking to get you there. Have a read of these four steps to receiving feedback and think about how you could use them.

1. Thank the person for giving you feedback. This signals that you are open to what they have to say (provided you are actually open!) and encouraging of feedback. This will mean the person is more likely to keep giving you feedback in future, helping you continue to grow.

2. Clarify your understanding. "Can I check I've understood correctly that the report format we're currently using is not working for you? Tell me more about that? What is not working? What needs improving?"

"Tell me more about that" and "Help me understand" are two golden things to say in feedback conversations, if not all conversations. It shows you want to listen, to understand, to know more. It is the exact opposite of a defensive reaction, where you do all the talking, justifying the way you already do things. This is humility showing up again (see Being Credible, page 117).

3. Move towards action. "Okay, so the issue is X, and it needs improving by us and changing to Y. How do we get started?" Notice the 'we' language here, which would best suit a process or way of collaborating. If the feedback is more directly about your behaviour and therefore something *you* need to change, then using the first person would make more sense. For example, "I can work on that by doing ABC. How does that sound to you?" Or if you're not sure how to improve, ask them, "I'm not sure exactly how I can go about making those changes. Do you have any ideas, please?"

4. Follow up. Have you improved? Are things better? Going back to the person who gave you the feedback to check-in signals two things. First, you care about improving, you want to get better. That says a lot of good things to your manager/client/colleague/partner. Second, it shows just how open and encouraging you are of ongoing feedback. As with the first point, you are likely to get more feedback from this person in future.

It strikes me you may have the following question in your mind.

Did you just write 'partner', Helen?

Are you *seriously* telling me you get feedback from your husband?!

Well, yes. Consider it one of the oddities of being married to a psychologist. He gets plenty of feedback too!

But the fact is, you get feedback from your friends and family all the time. We just might not label it as feedback in the same way that we would a performance review with a manager.

When my sister-in-law told me she found it annoying that I buy her Christmas presents, that was feedback.

When my mum commented that I only call her every three weeks (or two months), that was feedback.

Am I suggesting that you say, "Thank you for the feedback. Can I clarify my understanding...?" in these personal situations? Of course not. Though it might be funny to watch.

What you could do is take the time to listen and notice that you are being given feedback. Notice that someone is communicating to you something that they like, or something they don't like. And you could choose to act on that, to ask questions, to find out what would work better for them. That will improve your relationships.

If the thought of asking someone how good you are at X fills you with an unconfident panic or dread, then let's return to the most powerful starting point: Being Outcome-Focused.

What outcome could you achieve if you were even better at what you do? What benefits could that bring you?

If you want these things, then it's worth Being Brave and

asking for the feedback. And combining what you hear with the tips in Being Competent will help you build a complete, objective view of your ability levels and a plan to get even better.

Summary & Reflection

Why might feedback be useful for you? What outcome could you achieve if you were even better at what you do? What benefits could that bring you?

How could you respond to feedback next time you get some?
What would you like to think? What would you like to say?

Conclusion

Sometimes I wonder if it's just semantics.

You know, in those moments when my gremlins get the better of me and I wonder why I'm writing this book and whether it's any good and if my message makes sense and who would want to read it and will anyone benefit and will anyone buy it and what if they don't like it?

And yes, that sentence was meant to be that long. It shows you how exhausting the gremlins are.

I've called the book *Better Than Confidence* and explained why these tools are better than working on your confidence, but isn't the outcome the same? Is it just semantics? As long as you end up feeling good and doing good, who cares how you got there?

I take a breath and remind myself of these useful tools.

What outcome do I want?

I want you, dear reader, to thrive. To step out and do something new. To take a considered risk. To think about what you want and discover ways to overcome the gremlins that could hold you back. To help others do the same.

What is important to me about that?

That I tell you the truth. That I give you useful tools. And I know that the tools in this book are more useful than focusing on becoming more confident. How do I know? Mainly because I have seen these tools help so many people over my career, myself included. I have learnt many of these tools *from* my clients, as they have discovered their own better ways of thinking to get the outcomes they wanted.

You might wonder, if these tools are so good how come I'm still sitting here writing this book with so many gremlins and concerns?

Because these tools are for life. Because once you get rid of the gremlins in one part of your life, you may well find they appear somewhere new. And if and when they do, you'll need these ideas to shush the gremlins and find your courage.

I might have the gremlins, but I still wrote the book.

And perhaps that's a message to leave you with.

That the negative thoughts, fears and concerns are natural. They are part of our brain's self-protection system. We are unlikely to ever remove them completely, and if we did, that might be bad for our survival. So, when they appear and you find yourself doubting your ability and putting off doing something you wanted to do, here you have a guidebook to navigate your way through.

Waiting to feel confident first will waste your time.

Focusing on what you want will help you get there.

Where your gaze goes, you go.

Further Resources

available on helenfrewin.com

If you're looking for more now that you've read the book, here are some extra resources to keep you going!

In Part 1, I introduced the concept of the **Growth Mindset**. If you were interested in that and want to find out more, you could read Carol Dweck's book, or start with my summary of the book. I've added how I've seen the ideas used and abused since its release, and how you can make better use of the wisdom.

The Being Credible chapter contained suggestions on improving your impact through things like pace and tone. This is more easily demonstrated in a video than in a book, so have a look at the links to my videos on **Credibility & Impact**.

In Part 1, I introduced the grid of **confidence vs helpful thinking**. This is explored in more detail in an article I wrote to explain the concept and how you can monitor where you are for each given situation.

You can also download a follow-on e-book, *Better Than Confidence in Leadership*, written for people managers and HR/L&D professionals. Go to helenfrewin.com/offers.

Do you have questions I have not answered in the book? Let me know, because I'll be building an FAQs page. Contact me via helenfrewin.com.

About the Author

Helen Frewin is a business psychologist, executive coach, speaker and facilitator. She has worked in-house and as a consultant, advising companies on how to select talent, then develop and engage people to be at their best. Now a director at Totem, Helen is incredibly proud of her client list, which includes KFC, Disney, Dyson, Specsavers, Discovery, Kantar, Royal London, and various global law firms and banks.

An interview with Helen Frewin

What work do you do day-to-day?

About a third of my time is spent on selection-related projects, carrying out job analysis and advising companies on how to select the best people for those roles. The rest of my time is spent on my passion: developing people. Sometimes that's one-to-one coaching sessions, or it's in face-to-face or online workshops with groups of people. And then there's the speaker slots at conferences and events. The content I speak on varies from personal effectiveness and wellbeing to inclusive leadership and managing hybrid teams.

What inspired you to write this book?

I set out to write a book on honest conversations. That is a big passion of mine, as you might notice in the chapters on difficult conversations and feedback. When I help people to be more honest and get better outcomes, it's a good day for me. But every time I started writing, I couldn't get clear. I was lacking structure and getting lost. And then, in the week I was meeting with my publisher, the idea for this book hit me. How many people have been told they need more confidence? And with no idea what to do with that information, they wait and feel helpless. I see it all the time and I've got a load of tools that are better than confidence for addressing the blockers and gremlins we face. That was it, and two months later, the first draft was written.

What's next for you?

I have a goal of delivering a TED Talk on this subject, to spread the message as far and wide as possible that confidence is not the goal. Let's get more people engaging in more useful thinking. I also believe that the book on honest conversations will come back around. It's a passion that will not leave me any time soon. And in the meantime, I will be continuing to work with clients one-on-one and in groups, to make the world a more positive place, one conversation at a time.

What do you enjoy outside of work?

Walking in the Peak District, discovering new recipes, cocktails and restaurants with the husband, running (I need to do something to work off all the food), reading business, psychology and personal development books. Mostly relaxing at home in Leicestershire with the cutest cat on the planet.

How can people work with you?

One-to-one coaching, speaking, consultancy, workshop delivery, facilitation – the best starting point is to get in contact via helenfrewin.com. You can also find loads of free resources at totem-consulting.com.

Acknowledgements

When I read other people's books, I tend to skip over this bit. I'm not really interested in the author thanking the world, and I don't know any of the people they're talking about. But I had the privilege of being involved in a friend's book recently, supporting with editing, facilitating conversations and a launch event. What an incredible experience. And now, when I read her acknowledgements, it means so much to me to see my name there. It is recognition of the work and joy that went into supporting her. And now I'm doing the same – honouring those who have supported me on this journey.

Because it is a journey. An emotional one. A tough one. And I am incredibly grateful to everyone who has been a part of it.

To you, dear reader. I wrote this book for you. I wrote it in case it could help you on your journey. Tell me your story. Tell me what worked, what was useful, tell me what questions you still have at helenfrewin.com.

To Ellen Watts at Butterfly House Publishing for your

unending support. Your passion for this book has fuelled me when I was running on empty, and your expertise has been useful beyond words.

To Martha Hankins and Sarah Butler for believing in me and always being cheerleaders.

To Grace Marshall for inspiring me in every conversation, and in your incredible writing.

To Krush Makwana, an inspiration and evidently fuel for a fair few stories in this book. It is a privilege to work with you.

To the beta readers, you wonderful bunch of people, willing to read, edit, support and challenge me. Sarah Williams, Moni Holliday, Laura Barnes, Monique Knaapen, Jo Lipman, Caroline Milliken, Suzy Oklin, Kirsti Macqueen and Peta Young. Thank you for your openness, super useful feedback and support. You have made this book so much better than the first draft!

To the incredible clients I have the privilege of working with. Many of you have appeared in this book, under your name or under a pseudonym. You have been the inspiration for this book: your stories, your challenges and the transformational journeys we have been on together.

To the husband. It's one thing to say, "Sure, write a book, why not?!" It's quite another to be there for all the emotional rollercoasters along the way. Thank you for your perseverance and for the hugs when they were most needed. Twenty years in and I am still grateful every day that I married my best friend. Well, most days. We're still human.

And finally, Mum and Dad. I could not be here without the foundation you set for me. You told me to do my best, and that was always good enough for you. You gave me a soft cushion to land on when I fell and all the freedom I could wish for, so I could fly. Thank you.

Looking for more?

Wondering how you can use the ideas in this book with a team? If you are a people manager, leader or HR/L&D professional, then here's an offer for you. I've also written a follow up to Better Than Confidence, guiding people managers and HR teams on how to help their teams thrive:

BETTER THAN CONFIDENCE
In Leadership

And now that you have bought this book, you can also download the free e-book. Simply go to:

helenfrewin.com/offers

Download your free copy now.

Printed in Great Britain
by Amazon

82930188R00129